The Illusion of Excellence

And Other Seasonal Sermons

by

Eugene Brice

CBP Press
St. Louis, Missouri

Unless otherwise indicated, all scripture quotations are from the New Revised Standard Version Bible, copyrighted 1989 by the Division of Christian Education of the National Council of Churches of Christ in the United States of America.

Library of Congress Cataloging-in-Publication Data

Brice, Eugene.
The illusion of excellence, and other seasonal sermons.

1. Christian Church (Disciples of Christ)—Sermons. 2. Sermons, American. 3. Occasional sermons. I. Title.
BX7327.B74I45 1990   252'.066   90-35030
ISBN 0-8272-1609-2

The Illusion of
Excellence

For my children,
Mark, Deborah, Stephen, and David

Table of Contents

Introduction

Did the woman actually mean what she said? He thought so, because she said it with a perfectly straight face. Further, everything she added as she went on seemed to confirm her seriousness. "It would be so much better," she had said, "if Christmas just didn't come during the holidays!" All this had come up in a counseling session in which they had talked about unusual stress at her home.

But after she left, he sat thinking about it. "If Christmas just didn't come during the holidays!" As he thought about his own family schedule, he wondered if she didn't have something there. And not just Christmas! Add Easter to that list, and Thanksgiving, and the Fourth of July, and Mother's Day, and all the rest.

Getting matters at home arranged right is hard enough, but what does the preacher do with these special days that dot the church year, usually coming at holiday time? Often the preacher comes to church on those special Sundays with some badly mixed emotions. He knows that with the exception of the Big Three—Christmas, Easter, and Mother's Day—the attendance will probably be lower than usual. Many of the regulars will be away doing what the minister and family would like to be doing: visiting family, or going to the lake.

Not only must the minister be properly in place; she must also come up with some special approach that will tell the old story in some effective, listenable way. If the holiday is one of the nation's secular celebrations, the preacher must not let it utterly capture and run off with the gospel itself. Sometimes the activities that are traditional for the day convey the least important messages. (A corsage for the oldest, youngest, most prolific mother...!)

Despite these dangers, I have found that people look forward and are receptive to effective special-day sermons. The seventeen sermons that follow are offered in the hope that they will avoid the pitfalls and meet the challenges of those special days. In offering them here, I want to express appreciation to my wife and children, who stayed around on many a holiday weekend when they would have preferred to be elsewhere, and to my secretary, Marianne See, who took some of her own holiday time to type all this.

1 | *New Year's Sunday*

Danger: New Year Under Construction

Matthew 7:24-27

Every person here was given exactly 8,760 of them. You were given that many, and so was the person sitting beside you. The President was given that many, and so was Madonna and Joe Montana. 8,760! Are you wealthy? No difference there, you got no more than the poorest among us. The Equal Rights Amendment may not have been ratified but it is in effect here: Male and female, all got the same—8,760. And all of us here have already used up exactly 83 1/2 of them.

Hours! Eight thousand, seven hundred sixty hours this year. Time makes up the building blocks of this new year now under construction, and we are all absolutely equal in what we have been given: 8,760 hours, to do with as we will. The only difference is what we choose to do with them. And what an important difference this is, for given exactly the same set of circumstances, we can respond in a wide variety of ways.

The story from a generation or two ago tells of two fellows who were sent out into a remote part of the Ozarks to sell shoes. Almost immediately, one of the salesmen sent a telegram back to the home office. "Am returning at once," he wired. "Can't sell shoes here. Everyone goes barefoot." No word came from the other salesman for a few days, until a letter arrived at the home office. It came in a bulky, bulging envelope. The letter said: "Fifty orders enclosed. Prospects unlimited. Nobody here has shoes!"

Same situation, different interpretation! Same amount of time each of us is given, same world we live in, same people we work with, but what different results emerge from us. The annual coming of a new and fresh year highlights our assignment for us: to take this unused year now under construction and build something lasting and worthy from it. That is God's assignment to you and to me, put most simply. Opportunities beyond number, needs to be filled, growth to be reached for, and 8,760 hours to do it in, this building of a new year.

But recognize that there are dangers involved in such an effort. Hard hats are required around the construction site, for falling debris is frequent and mistakes are easy. Here on this first Sunday of the year, consider how these dangers affect you as you build your own new year.

Danger Number One is our excessive determination to hold on to the past and let it have too much voice in building this brand new year. By its very nature, building is a future-tense assignment. In his parable of the builder (Matthew 7:24ff.), Jesus' main point is the good builder's awareness of what the future might bring, and the foolish builder's disinterest in this. In the original Greek of this passage, the language conveys the understanding that the foolish man not only *built* his house on the sand but that he *kept on building* it there, a stubbornly continuing action. To supply too many details is to overwork Jesus' story, but the implication is there that the foolish builder was tied to that sandy site by the past, and despite its bad record as a place to build, was never willing to move away and try another place.

It's one of the dangers encountered in building a new year, that ghostly hand that reaches out from the past and knocks down anything that we try to build. It may represent loved ones whom we have lost; places we've lived that we like better than the present one; jobs we've had that have been taken away; children who have gone with the wind. A myriad of things reaches into our lives from the past, and grasps the reins of our life. One and all, they represent a past that will always be there in memory. But that past makes a most uncertain foundation upon which to build a future.

One of the most dramatic moments in the history of this hemisphere came in 1519 when Hernan Cortes landed his six hundred fifty men on the east coast of Mexico. Once they were ashore and all the supplies had been unloaded, Cortes ordered the ships burned. When hardships would develop on the expedition at hand, he did not want men whose attention was centered on easy trips back to Spain. That little company of men stood and watched those ships burn, knowing that any return to Spain would have to depend on new ships being built or new expeditions sent out.

In a symbolic way, every December 31 is a time when old ships are burned, and new expeditions are embarked upon. But there are so many people today who still *try to sail away in ships burned by time*, who stand looking across an ocean of years or miles to times and places that won't be again—unaware that even as they stand looking back, they are standing on the shore of a continent of time and opportunity grand beyond description, if only they will claim it.

But it requires future-tense thought to do it. The past is a treacherous foundation on which to build our house. It is tomorrow that we are going to be living in and living up, and if we want tomorrow to be any better than today, we have to plan for it. It will be just as miserable and as hopeless as we choose to make it, or it will be as joyful and exciting as we choose to make it. *We* choose the building site, and one danger we face is that we cannot turn loose of the past as we move on.

Dathane Stanley writes about her daughter who "came down the stairs one evening and said, 'Have you ever pushed and pushed on a door, and then discovered it was a wall?' She had turned off the light in her bedroom and then in the darkness tried to force open what she had mistakenly thought was a door."[1]

Doesn't that little story cause just a quick spark of recognition in all of us? *Pushing on walls!* Standing there, stubbornly, trying to make life something it isn't and can never be! Playing games with ourselves about the realities of life! We are game-playing people, aren't we? The sign

4

that was seen in the window of a loan company said, "Now you can borrow enough to get completely out of debt!" Pushing on walls, indeed!

To put it clearly: The past is a wall, not a door. The door is the future, and if we can realize this, we will have successfully dodged one real danger as we go on constructing this new year.

Danger Number Two is that we will be satisfied with too little as we build this new year. The provocative detail that Jesus leaves out of his parable of the builders is this: *Why* was the foolish builder content to build his house on such a questionable foundation? Why did he settle for so little? Did the past tie him to that one site, as we suggested a moment ago? Was it an expensive place, one that cost him nothing? Why did he settle for it? Jesus leaves this to our own imaginations, and wisely so, for no one reason would do for the builder, as no one reason will do for us.

Why do *we* settle for so little? Given these 8,760 hours, given these opportunities, given the fact that *we are going to be living* in this house we build, why do we settle for so little? The ironic point in the parable of the builders is that it takes just as much hard work to build a house on a poor foundation as it does on a good one. The work involved is basically the same. But the results are so vastly different. Clearly, one danger encountered in this new year under construction is our strange willingness to settle for so much less than we might in what we make of our lives.

While visiting a zoo one day, a certain man paused before the lion's cage, watched for a few moments, and was puzzled at what he saw. The lion's cage had recently been enlarged greatly and remodeled in order to give the animal more open, natural space. But strangely, the lion still paced back and forth within the smaller, now unseen, boundaries of his old cage as it was before enlarging. Back and forth he went, turning in the same place each time, where the wall once had been, ignoring all the extra space beyond. The animal's keeper wandered by and the visitor asked for an explanation. "Why does the lion pace back and forth in this narrow space, instead of exploring his new area?" The keeper answered quickly: "It's the same old story. The lion is busy making a cage of his own."

Busy making a cage of his own! Doesn't that capture some of us completely? Who says we have to build our house on sand? *We* do the choosing! Who says life has to be so constructed and narrow? When you awaken tomorrow morning, in that instant before you get up, who determines what kind of day it will be for you? Your boss, you say quickly? Not completely. Circumstances may choose the frame of the day, but you paint the picture that goes in it. If you choose nothing but blacks and grays, that's the picture you'll paint. But you do the choosing! And so many people, even as this new year begins, are already busy pacing up and down in little unwalled prisons of their own making, settling for so little.

It's a point that runs like a thread through all the teachings of Jesus. You are in charge of your life. You are not a helpless victim of circumstances; *you are in charge.* The prodigal son decided on his own to leave home, and then decided on his own to come back again. The good Samaritan decided to stop alongside that road between Jerusalem and Jericho. The wise builder decided to build his house on a rock. Each person is in charge of his or her own life.

Why is this such a hard fact for us to understand and accept? It must be hard for us to grasp, because so many of us are standing waiting for life to happen to us. We are waiting for something to happen to make us happy. We are waiting for someone to make us happy. We are waiting for that perfect set of circumstances to come along, people and places and things, and then life will be complete and full. Don't you believe it! Life is going to be just what you decide to make of it.

I challenge you at this moment to put this truth to work. You've taken the trouble to get here today, and you've listened well, so don't let this sermon go floating out into thin air. Right now, let there be some resolution within you, some specific goals set. One year from now, you'll be looking back on this year, used up and discarded. What do you want to see there as you look back? What goals and accomplishments do you want to have achieved? Set those goals high, and then aim at them, work for them. Good things seldom happen accidentally. They happen because someone thought about them and worked for them.

One point I often share with young couples sitting in my office talking about getting married is this: Ten years from now, what do you want to have happened in your married life together? What do you want your life to be like? If we could visit in your home a decade from now, what would you want us to see there? That is your goal, your destination you want to have arrived at ten years hence, and there is a road that leads inevitably to that destination, if you want to take it. Then don't just sit there waiting for a good marriage to happen to you! Work on it, plan for it, and aim high.

That truth applies to all of us, for we stand equal here. There are 8,760 hours in the new year, hours that will be filled up with all sorts of building material, jobs and assignments, friends and families, opportunities for learning and for growth. The one indisputable fact is that we *are* going to build *something* with all this, and one year from now, we will be living in that which we build.

So let the new year be abuilding, but be alert to the hazards. Don't let the past bind you down as you build. And don't let too limited a vision blind you. Perhaps Robert Sharpe's words sum it up:

Isn't it strange
That princes and kings,
And clowns that caper
In sawdust rings,
And common people
Like you and me
Are builders for eternity?

Each is given a bag of tools,
A shapeless mass,
A book of rules;
And each must make
Ere life is flown,
A stumbling-block
Or a stepping stone.[2]

Which will it be for *you* in this new year?

[1]*The Secret Place*, February 6, 1981.
[2]R. L. Sharpe, "A Bag of Tools."

2 | *Lent*

What's This About Lent?

Matthew 7:13-14

He came originally from a small town, and grew up in a rather conservative Protestant church there. Out of this background, he offered the question: "What's all this about Lent? I don't think I ever heard of it until I grew up. Is it new? We always had Christmas in our church, and Easter and Good Friday, but we never paid any attention to Lent. Where did it come from, and what's the point of it?"

On this first Sunday of Lent, that's a good question. Start by saying that the observance of Lent certainly isn't new. It's older than Christmas, in fact, starting back in the third century of the church's history. The word *lent* is first cousin to our word "lengthen," and bears a family resemblance. In the spring of the year, when days begin to lengthen, a period was set aside to lead up to Easter Sunday, the day of resurrection. Over a period of many years, the church settled on forty days as the length of that period. Lent begins on Ash Wednesday, the fortieth weekday before Easter, and officially concludes at noon on Saturday of Holy Week.

Why forty days? Moses was forty days on Mt. Sinai, receiving the Law. Jesus fasted forty days in the wilderness. According to some authorities, Jesus was in the tomb for forty hours, and there were forty days between the

7

resurrection of Christ and his Ascension. Whatever the reason, the church back in the third century chose to set aside a forty-day period before Easter as Lent, "days of lengthening." After the Protestant Reformation, many Protestants identified Lent not with the church but with Roman Catholicism, and abandoned its observance. In recent years, however, the value of Lent has been remembered, and it is receiving more attention among Protestants than ever before.

"All right," the questioner says, "that is its history. But what is its point? What does one do for Lent? I've always heard that you're supposed to give up something for Lent, and I hear jokes about people who give up cauliflower, or give up exercising, or even give up their New Year's resolutions. But I'm sure Lent calls for some specific response on the part of Christians. What is it?"

If there is one word that Lent forces on us, one word that characterizes its original purpose, it is the word "discipline." Lent has always been a time for getting oneself in line, of gathering up some loose ends of life. Discipline is not a popular concept in our day. Many of the commercials we watch on television point us in the other direction. "Pamper yourself," they tell us. "These cosmetics may cost a little more, but you're worth it." "You deserve a break today." The message we most often hear is "indulge yourself," and here comes a season of the Christian year saying "discipline yourself." Let's look more specifically at what a Lenten discipline means.

Discipline involves saying "No." We are most familiar with discipline as it makes this demand on us. Last Monday morning the phone rang at the church, and a young adolescent male voice asked if we had a Hot Line here at the church. He had a question he had to ask a minister, and he needed a quick answer. I happened to be the one who walked by at that point, so I got the call. The young man was not a member of this church, but for complicated reasons he called here first. He wanted a yes or no answer, and I invite you to decide how *you* would have answered him. Remember now, a simple yes or no. "I want you to tell me," he said, "is looking at Playboy and Penthouse magazine a sin, or not?"

I heard that question with great sympathy, and my heart yearned for that young man. He had all the normal urges of adolescence, but he had a conscience, and while something seemed awfully right about such magazines, something seemed awfully wrong as well. I could imagine—more than that, I could remember—the strong impulses that come in that age, the fear and eagerness mixed together in a dawning sexual awareness, the stumbling efforts to do both what is right and what is wrong, the pull from different directions. What a difficult assignment we give ourselves and our children here, to become aware of and adapt to urges and actions that move so quickly and inexplicably back and forth between the acceptable and the forbidden. And all this must take place in a setting where some witnesses say "anything goes" and others say "ain't it awful."

All this went through my mind quickly, sounding old echoes, as that young man asked his question. And I refused to give him a simple "yes" or "no." Whether what we talked about for five minutes or so was helpful to him or not, I don't know. But the gist of that conversation went like this: Every decision we make about things like this— what to read, where to go, what to do—is a door leading to something else, something more involved and complex. Little decisions are doors leading to certain rooms, and when we make the decision, we enter that room full of implications and dangers and possibilities and doors to other rooms. When you make a decision be sure you can handle what's in that room it leads to. The value of a simple and quick "No" to some temptation is that it guards you from all the tangled unknowns that act introduces. Someone has put it in short poetic form:

"Who's there?" I said. "A little lonely sin."
"Enter," I said, and all hell was in!

Lent is a time to practice saying "No" to some of those decisions that lead us to consequences we are not prepared to handle. It may be that a good discipline for each of us during Lent would be to identify a habit, a weakness in our lives that keeps getting us in difficult situations, and for forty days, at least, say "No" to it. Lent is a time of discipline, and discipline involves saying "No."

But discipline involves saying "Yes," too. One reason Lent fell out of favor for many people is that it came to be almost an orgy of gloom. Who could sacrifice the most? Who could subject the self to more denial and humiliation, even pain? But discipline involves not only saying "No" but also saying "Yes." Given the choice, when Lent begins I would rather see someone *take up* something than *give up* something.

We spoke a moment ago about little decisions being doors that lead to certain rooms, and we looked at that in terms of temptations that face us, and what ominous things they may introduce. But little decisions are also doors to rooms full of light and life and promise. Lent can be a period of choosing certain of those doors and going in them, and opening oneself to unexpected renewal there.

What might those doors be? Perhaps a daily devotional period, a time for reading of the Bible or other devotional literature. Perhaps a discipline of prayer—not just scattergun prayer, but prayer aimed at some specific purpose. Perhaps a discipline of affirming people about us—consciously looking for ways to affirm people who work with us or for us, or who live with us. Perhaps a discipline of gratitude—taking the trouble to call or write persons who today or years past entered our lives and we grew from it. Perhaps a discipline of physical exercise for those of us who do little more than bend our elbows as we eat. Perhaps a discipline of small gifts to people who are alone in the world with no one, no one at all to care. Perhaps a discipline of worship in our weekday Lenten services, or somewhere else. Perhaps a discipline of community service, as a volunteer in one of our great community agencies. Perhaps, if you have children at home, a discipline of "being there" to them for a time each day, really listening in a caring way. Perhaps a discipline of understanding—if we're conservatives we'll pledge to read Carl Rowan's column every day, and if we're liberals we'll read James J. Kilpatrick's column. We will seek to let Lent bring to us a lengthening of the mind and spirit, as well as of the days.

To repeat: Each one of those small disciplines is a door leading to rooms full of unexpected experiences and people. Discipline involves saying "No," but it also involves saying

"Yes," and Lent is a yearly reminder of our opportunities here.

And finally, *discipline helps us to see God.* Surely that's why Jesus in the Beatitudes put it as he did: "Blessed are the pure in heart, for they will see God" (Matthew 5:8). The fact that many people cannot see God does not mean God isn't there—it just means they can't see. Those who are pure in heart, Jesus said, those who have said "No" to some things and "Yes" to others, they are able to see God.

On any clear day, we could go outside and look up, and if our vision were keen enough, we could see the stars. The fact that we cannot see them doesn't mean they're not there. They *are* there, but our eyes see too many other things to pick them out. We see the haze in the air, the faint clouds, the blueness of the sky's atmosphere—we see so many things that we cannot see the stars shining in the distant skies. Our own lives get like that, cluttered up with so much that we cannot see God. Lent presents us with a time for discipline, a time for focusing our lives in on God, by saying "Yes" to certain things and "No" to others. Nothing ever gets done without this kind of focusing in on one goal. You can't write a letter or read a book or cook a meal without ignoring a thousand distractions. If any of us honestly want to see God in some special way this Lenten season, there's a whole series of "Yeses" and "Nos" that will get us there.

Jesus put it quite bluntly to those who would see God: "Enter through the narrow gate; for the gate is wide and the road is easy that leads to destruction, and there are many who take it. For the gate is narrow and the road is hard that leads to life, and there are few who find it" (Matthew 7:13-14). The narrow road of discipline leads to life. And that's what Lent is all about. For those who want to find life, who want to see God, it is a time for focusing in, and finding, and seeing.

Back in the early 1400s, when daring sailors were pushing farther and farther westward into the Atlantic, reports kept coming back of a beautiful set of islands out there called the St. Brendan Islands. The reports differed on where they were, but all agreed that they were out there somewhere. It was then that King Ferdinand of Spain, in

order to reward one of his sea captains, issued this procla-
mation: "I grant to Captain Vogado full title to the St.
Brendan Islands, *provided he can find them.*"

Did he ever find them? We don't know, but we never
hear of Vogado again. Perhaps he never went looking. But
provided he could find them, they were his. Are there times
in our lives when we really find God? God is here for us, all
about us and within us, provided that we find God. Lent is
a time for looking, for disciplining ourselves to see.

Bernard Lea Rice spoke for all of us in these words:

> I could see God tonight,
>   If my heart were right.
> If all the rubbish of my soul
>   Were cleared away, my being whole,
> My breast would thrill in glad surprise,
>   At all the wonder of my eyes.
>
> If my heart were right
>   I could see God tonight.
> And in the radiance of his face
>   I'd flame with light and fill this place
> With beauty and the world would know
>   The face of God down here below—
> Tonight!
>   If only my dull heart were right.

What's all this about Lent? Through helping us get our
dull hearts right, Lent helps us see God.

3 | *Palm Sunday*

The King Who Keeps Coming

Matthew 21:1-11

It was 1948, and my twin sister and I were high school seniors. Why we did it, I still do not really know. In all honesty, I have to say that we were more responsible than many teenagers, and usually could be counted on to be wherever we said we were going to be. At least eventually. Our parents had only a minimal amount of worry from us. And maybe that was what made it so anxious for them.

One Friday night, we were out with a half-dozen of our friends, engaged in a regular Friday-night outing. I cannot recall what the main event of the evening was, but what followed is remembered. We were always home soon after eleven from such outings, but on this particular night one of the group had his car, and so we started riding around. Now it really did not take much time to ride around our little town, but we rode everywhere, out into the country, through cemeteries, down farm roads, everywhere.

Somehow, it never occurred to us that anyone would be concerned. After all, *we* knew where we were, and that we were all right, and so we did not bother to call home. Midnight, one o'clock, two o'clock, and finally, it seemed enough to us, and we went home. We were genuinely surprised to find them up. How quickly a parent can change from sick anxiety to justified anger, from "Will I ever see my precious child again?" to "I ought to break your neck!"

Since midnight, our dad had been out in the car looking for us. Perhaps our paths in the cars had crossed, but he had come looking—looking in the movie theatre, which was always closed by 10:30 in our town, looking in the city park, looking down at the church recreation room, looking at friends' houses. He came to look for us.

On occasions since then I have driven into my hometown in the wee hours of the morning, and as I have gone through that deserted town, I have remembered how he drove those same dark streets, looking for us—how he kept coming.

There are times, of course, when love means waiting patiently, trusting to the movement of time for the bringing of an answer to our problem. The patience of God, our heavenly father, is often noted. If God wants a tree, God plants a seed and waits. If God wants a canyon, God starts a river flowing. If God wants a Savior, God brings to birth a baby.

But in that love for us, God does more than wait. God keeps coming. Persistently, quietly, God keeps coming to us, and this was precisely the strategy of Jesus, "in [whom] God was reconciling the world to himself" (2 Corinthians 5:19). On this Palm Sunday we remember the coming of Christ the King into Jerusalem, but always he has been the King who *keeps coming*.

Have you ever noticed the persistence with which Christ kept coming to people in his brief ministry? He came to them in the day-to-day activities of life, not forcing himself upon them, but being there, and confronting them with his presence.

• There was the wedding feast in Cana of Galilee to which he came, and when the worried father of the bride ran out of wine, Jesus reached out, and there was wine aplenty. A small child heard the story of this first miracle that Jesus performed, at the wedding feast in Cana, and was asked what she learned from it. "I guess," she said, "it means that if you have a wedding, it's a pretty good idea to have Jesus there too." There were moments of joy and celebration like this, and in them, the King kept coming.

• He came in worship. They gathered for the Sabbath service in Nazareth, and he rose and read the scriptures and their hearts burned with his presence.

• There were times of sickness when he was there. So many who were ill, crippled, afraid, felt his shadow fall upon them, or touched the hem of his garment, or felt his hand on their brow, and they knew that the King had come.

• He came in darker moments as well. The Centurion's son lay near death. Mary's and Martha's brother Lazarus had already been gone a day or two, and in those moments of grief, Jesus kept coming, and touching with his presence those who were hurting.

• Some were busy at work, but he came to them. Mending their nets, some fishermen were; others, out in their boats fishing. Matthew was collecting taxes at his office by the streetside in Capernaum. Zacchaeus, the businessman, was up in a tree watching a parade. Busy people, all of them, and he kept coming to them.

• Most remarkable of all, he kept coming even when he was rejected time and again. There in the last weeks of his life the signs had all been bad. Many of the crowd had turned away from him; some had turned on him. The Pharisees were plotting ways to kill him, and the Sadducees were joining in. The Romans were always alert to and suspicious of any troublemakers, and Jesus saw all this. He knew that the clouds were gathering, that the storm was coming, that death was imminent—but he kept coming.

Up to Jerusalem he went, to the walled city filled with those who were the most antagonistic to his work, to the most dangerous place of all. To the center of the worst hostility, the fiercest hatred, the most certain rejection, he came. And as a King he entered into that City of David, with scarcely a glance at the hill of Calvary outside the wall. He was, to the very end of his life, the King who kept on coming.

Is it surprising, then, that he keeps coming to us today? "Remember, I am with you always," he said, "to the end of the age" (Matthew 28:20), and through this promise, he keeps coming.

He comes to us in moments of rich joy, in moments when the ordinary water of life has been turned into wine. Like the disciples to whom he came, we know that it is the King who has come to us because our hearts "have been strangely warmed." He comes to us, then, when we feel love to be more than just a word in our homes, when we are deeply touched by someone's unselfishness, when the fresh beauty of a spring morning sings of new life in our hearts. If you are blessed with such moments as these, it is the King who keeps coming.

He comes to us in the passage of time, when we see the quickness of life and how fast it is rushing by us. When we see our baby boy now six feet tall and with a bushy black beard, when our college roommate turns out to have a grandchild, when what we hear with and chew with and see with all spend the night on the table beside the bed, we are reminded that time is moving quickly, that it runs out on us. In any experience of life that brings the message, "Work, for the night is coming when we work no more"— in any such experience, the King keeps coming.

And, strangely, he comes to us even in our worst moments. Just as he rode that Sunday into a hostile city, so he comes right into the walled city of our heart, where a part of us spreads garments and a part of us builds crosses. Right into our very worst moments he keeps coming, right into our stubbornness and selfishness, right into the darkest corners of our lust and greed, right into our repeated refusal to accept him, he keeps coming. "Neither do I condemn you. Go...and do not sin again" (John 8:11).

Do you see what this means? *It means that we do not have the power to stop his coming.* We can permanently reject the attentive love of a friend, but not *his* love. Turn him down repeatedly, yes! Give the reins of our lives over to our lowest selves, yes! Waste our lives in some nearby foreign land, yes! But even as we sit there in the pigsty of our own making, even there, he keeps coming! Remember how the Psalmist put it?

> Where can I go from your spirit?
> Or where can I flee from your presence?
> If I ascend to heaven, you are there;
> if I make my bed in Sheol, you are there....

If I say, 'Surely the darkness shall cover me,
and the light about me become night,'
even the darkness is not dark to you.
                    Psalm 139:7-8,11-12a

Even in sin and darkness, he keeps coming.

One of the grandest Christmas poems ever written came out of this fact of the persistence of God, the way in which God simply will not abandon us to the darkness of life.

It was in the late 1800s that a boy named Francis grew up in Manchester, England. Having felt a pull toward ministry, Francis had applied for admission to a Roman Catholic seminary to study for the priesthood. Because of his excessive shyness, he was turned down. For a while he went on to college, studying medicine but indifferently. His real interest, which he never confessed to his physician father, was poetry. While he was in his early twenties his mother, who had always encouraged him, suddenly died, and Francis' world crumbled about him. He went to London and joined the street people there, sharing all the worst that life could offer, from alcohol to opium.

But something kept stirring within and pulling at him. Through all this dark night of the soul, it would not let him go. One night, under a lamp post, he scribbled an essay on a piece of paper and sent it, along with some brief poems, to the editor of an English magazine. The editor noted the griminess of the envelope and stuck it in a drawer, unopened. Six months later, when he chanced upon it, he quickly recognized in its contents the mark of genius. He made efforts to find the writer, who by now had moved on without a trace. The editor published the poetry anyway. Months later, Francis Thompson saw them, went to the editor's office and identified himself as the fledgling poet.

The editor saw great potential in him, wasted as he was, and guided him to the care of a Christian home in London. Francis eventually conquered his opium addiction, entered a church school, and emerged a short time later as the writer of the famous Christian poem, "The Hound of Heaven." How well it expressed his deep feeling that through every dark night, God had been persistently, stubbornly, unceasingly on his tracks, never giving up the chase. It begins with these haunting words:

I fled Him, down the nights and down the days;
  I fled Him down the arches of the years;
I fled Him down the labyrinthine ways
  Of my own mind; and in the mist of tears
I hid from Him, and under running laughter.
    Up vistaed hopes I sped;
    And shot, precipitated,
  Adown titanic glooms of chasmed fears,
From those strong Feet that followed, followed after.

Through every moment of his sojourn through the far country, the King had kept coming to him.

Palm Sunday speaks to us of this stubborn King who pursues us through every experience of life, entering the walled city of our hearts and offering life to our death, and light to our darkness, and refusing to let our repeated turnings away be the final answer.

So, I say, he keeps coming to you today, and neither you nor I shall stay that coming until the day we die. He comes in our joy, in the excitement of new life, in moments of insight and meaning. He comes in our anxiety and our pain, never leaving us without comfort. He comes in our worst sin, seeing our stubborn disobedience, but never leaving us without hope. *Our father still drives the darkened streets of our lives looking to bring us, his late and lost children, back home again.*

To say it clearly: Too many of us live in the back roads of life, and we don't see him looking. But he keeps on searching, persistently. He keeps after us, and those strong feet keep following after. The gospel's grandest news is that on that Palm Sunday long ago, and in these sacred moments today, our Savior, Jesus Christ, is always the King who keeps on coming.

4 | *Easter Sunday*

The Man with the Second Chance

John 11:1-4, 38-44

Just suppose that you were suddenly given a second chance with life, a chance to start all over again. What would you do with it? Would there be any difference between your first effort and your second?

Most of us know some things we would want different if we started over again, and many of those things relate to our appearance. Surveys show that nine out of ten of us have concerns about our appearance, and wish something were different, or at least arranged differently. Young adults are most apt to want something changed—weight or height or skin or hair—and as we grow older, the fewer complaints we have about ourselves. But if we were, indeed, starting over, we could list some things we would want different.

But what would we *do* that is different? How many of us long for a second chance in a given situation that didn't come out right. The basketball player takes the final shot, with four seconds left in the game, and he misses; the game is lost. We know what second chance *he* would like to have. Several years back, the Dow Jones Industrials Average hovered around 1200, and the broker advised selling out and going liquid. Now the market flirts with 3000 and the broker wishes he had a second chance. "If I knew then what

I know now," we say, "it would be different." We remember an argument we had with someone, and in cool retrospect we say, "What I should have said to her was..." Someone has put this predicament in poetic terms:

Backward, turn backward, oh time in your flight,
I thought of a comeback I needed last night.

That's when we think of them, and we would like a second chance.

And sometimes, more seriously, that yearning for a second chance comes in the midst of some life-threatening situation. We didn't know there was ice on the road, and the car goes into one of those sickening skids. We say, "Dear God, get me out of this. Another chance!" An unexpected health problem prompts a physical examination, and a lab report is prepared. Here comes the doctor with the results and we breathe a prayer: "Dear God, another chance, please. Just get me through this, and it will be different from now on."

Most of us have seen those television insurance commercials that show some ordinary citizen plucked out of a busy life and suddenly heading upward on a heavenly escalator—clamoring for a second chance. "Wait a minute," the frantic fellow exclaims, "I've got a wife and kids. I haven't done my income taxes yet. Get me out of here!"

Now picture yourself in that predicament. The escalator is on its way up with you on it. But suddenly, inexplicably, something happens to give you a second chance at life. The escalator reverses itself and brings you back down again. That is what happened to the man whose death caused Jesus to paint the grandest of all pictures of himself: "I am the resurrection and the life" (John 11:25).

His name was Lazarus. He was obviously a very special friend of Jesus, for when they brought word of his illness they said to Jesus, "Lord, he whom you love is ill" (11:3). Lazarus, citizen of Bethany, brother of Mary and Martha, lay dying, and Jesus, it was said, should come at once.

It was two days before Jesus could get there, and by the time he arrived in Bethany, Lazarus was dead. Martha met Jesus and spoke her grief: "Lord, if you had been here, my brother would not have died. But even now I know that

God will give you whatever you ask of him." Jesus said to her, "Your brother will rise again." Martha said, "I know that he will rise again in the resurrection on the last day" (11:21-24).

It was then that Jesus painted for her this final picture of himself. "Martha," he said, "I am the resurrection and the life. Those who believe in me, even though they die, will live, and everyone who lives and believes in me will never die" (11:25-26). He then proceeded to the tomb where his friend Lazarus lay, and there beside the tomb, in the Bible's shortest verse, "Jesus wept" (11:35, RSV). Then, for reasons that remain unclear to us, Jesus called into the re-opened tomb, and the miracle was performed. The escalator was reversed, and Lazarus came back for a second chance at life.

How did they all feel about this? The bystanders were amazed, of course, and some became believers in Christ because of what they saw. Mary and Martha were over-joyed, and probably, but not certainly, most of the rest of Lazarus' family were also. There was probably a nephew somewhere who had to hand back Lazarus' gold watch, and there were others who had adjusted almost too well and almost too quickly to a life without Lazarus. But all in all, they received Lazarus back gladly.

And Lazarus? How did *he* feel about it? No one had asked him whether he wanted to come back or not. We have many testimonials from persons who have had borderline death experiences, and they say that there is an ethereal joy felt in that movement through death, a sublime feeling of peace about it. Maybe Lazarus was not as happy about his coming back as his sisters were.

But the fact is that he *was* back, given a second chance by Jesus, the chance that many of us in our emergency moments pray for. *And what did Lazarus do with it?* Do you suppose that "Lazarus, Volume Two," was any different from "Lazarus, Volume One"? Was he kinder to his sisters, more tolerant to people, more willing now to give himself to the work of the Kingdom?

If he was different, the difference lasted no longer than an April snow. Lazarus was the only man in history to have been given a second chance, brought back from death, and you know what? *We never hear another word about Lazarus!*

We fantasize so much about what *we* would do with a second chance that this seems strange. When some life-threatening situation has us clinging to life, we talk much about second chances and "if only" and "what if." "Those chances I've wasted! Dear God, if I just get another chance, you're not going to recognize me. You'll think it is someone else. Just give me another chance, and you'll see."

Thinking like this about Lazarus, it is easy to picture him becoming one of Christ's strongest followers. We'll see him at the front of the line from now on, this man with the second chance. He'll be in Jerusalem, preaching in the Temple, and standing before the crowd there, defending Christ. What a follower, what a leader, this Lazarus will be!

But the strange fact is that we never hear Lazarus mentioned again! He wasn't one of those at the cross, when Jesus died. His sisters, these one-chance women, were there, but not Lazarus, their brother with a second chance. At the day of Pentecost a few months later when the church was established, there is no reference to Lazarus. He is not mentioned once in the Book of Acts, where the exciting history of the early church is described. He wasn't among the disciples, or the apostles, or the missionaries—he just disappears, taking his second chance with him into easy oblivion.

It causes me to think about my own instinctive yearning for second chances. Would *I* be any different from Lazarus? I picture myself in that television commercial. The service here is ending, and all of you are filing sadly out to leave, murmuring among yourselves, but I'm not among you. I'm watching you leave from the escalator—which is, I trust, upward bound. And I'm protesting every inch of the way. There's my family, my friends, so much I wanted to say, to do, and I want a chance, a second chance, to file some returns of many different sorts. And suddenly it happens for *me*! The escalator shudders and stops and comes back down and deposits me right here, with my mouth still working furiously. Another chance for me! *Would it be different?*

Would it be different for you? Be honest now: If you had a second chance at life, how different would it be? What would you do with that second chance? A clue to help you answer:What are you doing with all those second chances you are getting right now? Today was a second chance, yesterday was, and tomorrow will be: What are we doing with *these* second chances? Jesus said, "I am the resurrection and the life—*the life!*" "I came that [you] may have life, and have it abundantly" (John 10:10). Those of us whose dip into life is so shallow, would *we* dip any deeper if we had another chance? Those of us who love so little, who give so little, who think so little: What about *today* as a day of resurrection and life? "Today is the first day of the rest of your life," the saying goes, and it's a day for all those of us who yearn for second chances but don't take advantage of the one we have already here and now.

But there is a further question for us: Where *is* Lazarus? Didn't Jesus raise him from the dead? What *did* happen to him? Lazarus died, of course. He died again, and set out on that journey once more. This is my theory of why Lazarus didn't amount to much in his second-chance lifetime. Having heard echoes of heavenly music in that first brief excursion into death, Lazarus spent the rest of his life listening, waiting, anticipating. That's probably why we are, for the most part, kept ignorant about that life to come. It only takes a glimpse of heaven to make earth, with all its attractions, seem but a rest stop to be endured before moving on.

Lazarus died again, and again the picture Jesus painted of himself shines in our darkness. Not only abundant life here, abundant life to come: the best second chance of all! "I am the resurrection and the life." "I go to prepare a place for you....I will come again and take you to myself" (John 14:2-3). Those are the words for all of us, because however well we deal with the second chances of this life, we come finally to that chasm which brings it all to a close. No one can get across a chasm in two jumps, and especially this one. All our energy and skill and smartness can't do it. But through Christ, his life and his death and his resurrection, God comes bridging that chasm. Here in this glorious season of springtime and new birth, God comes giving us the best second chance of all.

Christ is the Lord of the second chance, giving us a myriad of new opportunities to make this life count for something, beginning right now. And then, as he paints this final picture of himself, he offers us the best of all second chances: "I am the resurrection and the life. Those who believe in me, even though they die, will live, and everyone who lives and believes in me will never die" (11:25-26).

On this resurrection morning, all praise to the God of the second chance.

5 | *Mother's Day / Christian Family Sunday*

The Hardest Gift to Give

John 8:31-36

Joe and his daughter Linda go shopping together. Of course their interests are different, so after they arrive at the store, Joe heads for the hardware section, and Linda looks for her own things. She looks at some clothes, examines the luggage, and then goes outside to see what's going on there. Joe and Linda finally rejoin forces, and return home, the shopping trip over.

Is that a good story or a bad one? It's a bad one, with real trouble barely averted, because Linda is only three years old. What she needed from her dad was the gift of a caring, protective love.

Here's another setting. Mary, the mother, gives that protective love in abundance to her son Jimmy. She notices if Jimmy's face looks flushed, or if he seems to be too thin, or if his shirts don't look neat and clean. She frequently cooks his favorite dishes, and keeps up on his friends and their character. She shows that caring love in many ways.

So we ask again, is this a good story or a bad one? It's a bad one, with real trouble brewing, because son Jimmy is 32 years old and married, and what he needs from his mother is the gift of freedom.

Here in these two settings, neither of them farfetched, we see reflected the difficulty of the role the Christian

25

family is called by God to play. You see, when God decided to create people, God created families to do it. Families are people factories, and production isn't easy. It isn't easy because the family is called on to do two sets of things entirely at odds with one another. Families must hold on to their offspring, but they also must let them go. They must carry them gently, but also teach them to walk by letting them stumble and fall.

Protecting and releasing, holding on and letting go, bringing in and turning out: all are functions of the family. We spend hours playing games with little spoons, getting them to eat mashed liver and strained spinach and egg yolk, and then watch them devour Big Macs and anchovy pizzas. We shudder as they take timid steps from coffee table to sofa, and then watch them skateboard down Trail Ridge Road. It's all there in the family role—the gift of love, the gift of freedom, each pulling in its own direction.

The best gift is the gift of love, no doubt about it. And that gift is central in our minds on this Mother's Day. We call it Christian Family Sunday and our emphasis *is* on the Christian family. But it's Mother's Day, most of all, and because we have one and all been recipients of so much, our memories work overtime.

• I remember awakening chilled as a youngster as someone stood by the bed pulling covers up over me. I remember the feeling of settling down into the warmth of those covers with the dim awareness that someone cared.

• I remember recuperating from a childhood illness as she brought soft-boiled eggs and toast, a meal that somehow in my mind is *still* so connected with getting well that it can cure almost anything I have.

• I remember a cold wash cloth brought and laid on my forehead to combat a frequent and painful headache. I remember sitting at the kitchen table, having just arrived late at night from college, and eating a meal she quickly put together.

• I remember fierce maternal words of consolation to me after a college romance went awry. "She's not good enough for you anyway! You can do better than her!" Somehow those words seemed to help, although I knew full well that up to then I *hadn't* done better than her, and considered myself lucky to have done that well at all. Still, it wasn't logic I needed then, but caring, and her words helped heal the hurt.

So many memories. And you share them—all of us do. Memories of love given from both father *and* mother—tender, protective love. What a great gift the family gives. A place to come home to. A place where we can relax and be accepted for what we are, where we do not need to play games or act out roles or pretend to be something we are not. A place where someone covers the bases we leave unguarded, where someone turns off the burners we leave on, and awakens us when we oversleep, and locks the doors at night and puts the milk back in the refrigerator and keeps the clothes washed, and all the rest.

Surely all this explains our strong emotions on this day:We have deserved so little but received so much, from this best gift of love—and our mothers symbolize as well as embody that gift.

But there comes a time when this gift becomes insuf-ficient, and a harder gift must emerge out of it. The best gift may be love, but *the hardest gift for the family to give is freedom.* An unselfish, serving love, a love which cleans up our messes and straightens out our mistakes and glues together our broken dreams: That love must give way to a love which turns loose and lets us go. Just as God's great gift to us, God's children, is freedom, so must it be the family's gift too—the family's hardest gift.

When the family does not grant this gift, the result is offspring who cannot mature into fulfilled, self-sufficient people. Some time ago, *The Atlantic Monthly* carried an article called "The Ruination of the Tomato." As a devotee of *real* tomatoes, and a hater of what's been made available in the supermarkets, I read the article closely. It seemed almost a parable of the family.

Modern technology brought it all about. Processors thought that tomatoes ought to have more solid material, have less acid, be smaller. Engineers called for tomatoes that had tougher skins and wouldn't roll off the conveyor belt. Growers wanted more tonnage to the acre, resistance to cracking. Market people wanted tomatoes that would turn red earlier, whether they were ripe or not. So they developed a spray that would force the tomatoes to turn red prematurely. They bred tomatoes for thick walledness, less acidity, more uniform ripening, oblongness and high yield. The only thing they had to sacrifice was flavor. But flavor was secondary, and now, thanks to modern technology, we can have year round a beautiful, red, thick-walled, oblong, firm—and utterly tasteless—tomato!

There are styles of family living that produce children like this. There are forms of government in our world that, in the name of big-brother benevolence, produce citizens like this. All the taste is gone, and all the freedom that produce art and music and literature and life's creative spontaneity. In so many settings, freedom is the hardest gift to give.

With our families, the big question is this: *At the proper time and with the proper balance, can our love change its strategy and turn loose?* The best gift is love. The hardest gift is freedom. Why is it so hard to turn our children loose and give them freedom?

It's hard because we've been programmed all these years to be protective. Look at the questions that occupy us as we bring new young lives into the world—questions that are the marks of our love:

"When can we bring him home from the hospital?"
"Is the bottle too hot?"
"Is she covered up?"
"Does his ear still hurt?"
"Did you close the backyard gate before he went out to play?"
"Did you fix the chain on his bicycle?"
"Is there a good first-grade teacher in that school?"
"Can we let her walk home from school?"
"Should she have a car date at fifteen?"
"It's 1:30! Hasn't he come in yet?"
"Did you send the college the tuition money?"
"When are we going to meet her family, son?"
"Are the wedding invitations addressed yet?"

(Now, right at this point the gift must be given completely! It has started long before, but right now the hardest gift has to be laid fully and finally beside the china and the silver—or else our list of questions will lead us straight to the ruination of the family!)

"Hasn't she sent her thank-you notes yet?"

"Can't you come over for dinner Friday night?"

"Aren't you ever coming to our house for Christmas?"

"Can't you get him to at least *ask* for a transfer back here?"

"Aren't you *ever* going to have children of your own?"

(And then, finally:)

"What do you mean, you *asked* for a transfer to Anchorage?"

All our lives, you see, our love has asked these questions. All our lives we've guarded and watched, made decisions for them, answered questions for them. No wonder it is hard to give them the same gift God has given us: freedom!

It's hard, too, because we are afraid for them. We see the rope loosening and their frail little boats slipping out into the waters much more troubled than *we* ever knew when we were their age. We are afraid for them. We don't want them hurt, and we look out there and see so many jagged edges. If we could only give them the benefit of our knowledge and experience, without their having to suffer as we did to get it.

The poet put it this way:

> Youth should heed the older-witted
>   When they say, Don't go too far—
> Now their sins are all committed,
>   Lord, how virtuous they are![1]

The poet has us right. Our sins are committed, our mistakes already made, and we would impose our virtues, our knowledge, on them. But still and all, that virtue and knowledge is born out of pain and suffering, and if we could only spare our children what we have gone through. They have to make so many huge decisions—from bitter experience, we know! So in our desparate, meddling ways, we keep holding on:

"Do you really want to major in that? Can you get a job with that kind of degree?"

"Son, do you think you really know her well enough to make a decision right now?"

"What? You're returning Bill's ring? The engagement is off? We always thought Bill was just right for you." (Somehow through all generations it remains an unlearned lesson: There is nothing like parental enthusiasm to kill any romance, and nothing like parental opposition to keep it going!)

It is hard for us to turn them loose, because we don't want to see them hurt.

Face the fact, too that *it is hard to give freeom because, quite frankly, many of us tend to be manipulators,* finding our own meaning in life by subtly, or openly, directing the lives of others—starting with our own children! We have been speaking primarily of the family here, but the point holds true in all our relationships, whether we are a husband or wife with no children, or right in the midst of a growing family, or living alone. One of our temptations is to find ways to manipulate people around us.

In *Man the Manipulator* Everett Shostrom defines the two relationships we can have with ourselves and others. We can manipulate, using all sorts of little games to do it, or we can actualize. To actualize means to grant ourselves and others the freedom to be and do what is inside us, to carve out of this raw material a life that will be productive and satisfying. To be an actualizer is to grant freedom. And it is the hardest gift the family is called on to give.

In short: God has chosen to use families to bring us into being and there we experience God's love for us. But that best gift of love leads to the highest, and hardest, gift of freedom. "You will know the truth," said Jesus, "and the truth will make you free" (John 8:32). Families that really work, families that really love, produce children who can claim that freedom. For the more successful the parents have been in loving, the more successful the child will be in leaving, and claiming life in abundance. And the more successful parents will have been in giving the hardest gift to give!

[1]Wilhelm Busch , "Pious Helen." Translated by Christopher Morley.

6 | *Baccalaureate Sunday*

Dealing with Failure

2 Corinthians 4:7-12

On the eve of your greatest accomplishment to date, I want to think with you about failure.

It was the biggest moment of his young career. Every eye was on him as he stood in that packed auditorium to announce his school's vote on a new president for the State Student Council Convention. A representative from each school across the state would stand and shout out, "Mr. President, Central High casts its vote for...," and then announce the city or school it was voting for.

His own school was near the end of the alphabet, and a close race had developed between Amarillo and Galveston as the next president. The lead see-sawed regularly, and each vote was listened to anxiously. Finally it came to his school, and he was spokesperson. Would the vote be for Amarillo, or Galveston? He stood nervously and said in a loud voice: "Mr. President, Sulphur Springs casts its vote for Sulphur Springs!"

He knew at once that he had misspoken, and tried quickly to regain his composure with a correction. But the roar of confusion and laughter that rose up from 1500 high-spirited young delegates drowned him out. The correction was finally made, with equal parts determination and embarrassment, and he shrank into his seat.

That incident happened to me forty-seven years ago last month, and I still remember it in incredible detail. I do not remember for whom I was supposed to be voting. I don't even remember who finally won. But I remember my moment of failure with a vividness that astonishes. Failure! It's a common denominator of every individual who ever even tried to accomplish anything at all.

Not long ago, I read about an incident in President Truman's life after he had retired and was back in Independence, Missouri. He was at the Truman Library, talking with some elementary-school children, and answering their questions. Finally, a question came from an owlish-looking little boy: "Mr. President, was you popular when you was a boy?" "Why, no," the President replied. "I was never popular. The popular boys were the ones who were good at games and had big, hard fists. I was never like that. Without my glasses I was blind as a bat, and, to tell the truth, I was kind of a sissy. I guess that's why I'm here today." The little boy started to applaud, and then everyone else did as well.

And so did I, as I read the story, for it is a reminder that each of us experiences failure in different ways. That's why Paul's words in 2 Corinthians have always hooked themselves into my mind. The J. B. Phillips translation puts it: "I have been knocked down, but not knocked out" (4:9). Because such moments come to us, we look for good news about failure.

Let's begin by noting that *failure is something we can avoid*. That is good news, isn't it? Failure is something we can avoid by saying nothing, doing nothing, being nothing.

I'm going to brag on myself a bit. I have never in my life choked up while singing a solo. I have never lost a match in a tennis tournament. I have never had a poem rejected by a literary magazine. I have never been defeated in a race for public office.

Inasmuch as I am one who loves music and tennis and poetry and politics, that's an amazing record. But, you see, I have never sung a solo. Or played in a tennis tournament. Or submitted a poem to a magazine. Or run for public office. I have never failed at any of these things because I have never tried.

Only those people who try something run the risk of failure. The main choice most of us make, the most important choice, is: At what level do we fail? I read recently of a speech given at Texas Christian University. The title of the speech reached out and grabbed my attention: "On Failing at a Very High Level." Each of us chooses the level of our failing. In baseball, some make major league errors, some make minor league errors, some make little league errors—and some don't make any errors at all, because they don't play the game.

Start, then, by being honest about failure. If you are able to be satisfied in life with saying nothing, doing nothing, and being nothing, failure will be avoided.

So let's move on to recognize that *failure is a teacher,* the best one we'll ever have. Consider this: The only way you ever learned to walk was by failure. If your first step had waited until you were sure you wouldn't fall, you'd still be wearing knee pads and high-topped white shoes with unscarred soles. The only way you ever learned to read, or add, or play the piano, or operate a computer was by trying it and failing and then trying again.

Last summer at Estes Park, in the court next to ours, some nine-year-olds were trying to play tennis. It wasn't going too well for them. One of them swung at the ball and hit it clear over the fence just as his mother walked by. "Throw the ball to us, will you, Mom?" the boy asked. She replied: "Why'd you hit it over the fence? You've had a tennis lesson!"

It takes more than a lesson in tennis to learn how not to hit it over the fence. It takes long practice and frequent failure. You don't learn to hit it in until you've hit it out many a time. In any area of life, failure is a first-rate teacher. Sir Humphrey Davy, the nineteenth-century physicist, put it this way: "The most important of my discoveries have been suggested to me by my failures."

For years, astronomers knew the planet Neptune existed, but they couldn't see it through their telescopes. They applied the math of Sir Isaac Newton and finally located it. Next they became stymied in their search for Pluto. According to Newton's laws of physics, it ought to be there—but it didn't show up where they thought it should be. For forty years, their searching was unproductive. Then along came Albert Einstein, who used the failure of Newtonian physics in the astronomers' searching for Pluto as a clue to help him devise the theory of relativity. One person's failure led to another's success.

Failure is a teacher, and it becomes an asset to us if we learn from it. We may learn that our present strategy won't work. We may learn that our goal itself wasn't good. We may learn that our inner problems interfere with outer work. We may learn that we quit too soon. Whatever it is, failure teaches us if we will let it.

Therefore, *no failure need ever be final!* Failure does not automatically mean defeat. Mary Pickford said, "If you have made mistakes, even serious ones, there is always another chance for you. What we call *real* failure is not the falling down, but the staying down." But no failure ever need be final, unless we declare it so.

Consider the whimsical response of the high school senior who had received a letter of rejection from the college he wanted to attend. "Dear Admissions Officer," the student wrote, "I am in receipt of your rejection of my application. As much as I would like to accommodate you, I find I cannot accept it. I have already received four rejections from other colleges, and this number is, in fact, over my limit. Therefore, I must reject your rejection, and will appear for classes on September 18."

Crazy as it is, I like that! It may not have worked for that student, but it has worked and it works in many a life. That's just what Paul did. The world stamped "failure" on his hand, and Paul erased it. "Knocked down, but not knocked out." *"I reject your rejection!"*

Any one of us can say that, too. So many have said it, and have risen from failure to real achievement. In 1902, the poetry editor of *The Atlantic Monthly* returned a sheaf of poems to a 28-year-old poet with this curt note: "Our magazine has no room for your vigorous verse." The poet was Robert Frost, who rejected the rejection. In 1905, the University of Berne turned down a Ph.D. dissertation as being irrelevant and fanciful. The young physics student who wrote the dissertation was Albert Einstein, who rejected the rejection. In 1894, the rhetoric teacher at

Harrow in England wrote on the 16-year-old's report card, "a conspicuous lack of success." The 16-year-old was Winston Churchill, who rejected the rejection.

So let's sum it up.

• You *can* avoid failure—by saying nothing, doing nothing, being nothing.

• If you *do* try and occasionally fail, use it as a teacher, and learn from it.

• No failure ever need be final. *No* failure, none at all, ever need be final.

God bless you as the adventure begins.

7 | *Memorial Day*

Some Things to Forget on Memorial Day

Philippians 3:12-16

We were on vacation, heading west out of Albuquerque when we noticed signs pointing southward to the Acoma Pueblo, one of the few continuously occupied pueblo villages in the West. The travel books said it was worth seeing, so we turned off the highway, pulling behind us a good-sized, fold-down tent trailer. A mile or two later, we saw the pueblo occupying the entire top of a mesa. There was a parking area at the foot of a narrow dirt road that circled steeply to the top where the village was.

How would we get up? We would drive up, I said. "Oh, it's too steep. You can't get up there pulling a trailer," my wife said. "You can't get up that steep road," my son said. "You can't drive up there," my daughter said. "Sure I can," I said. "Haven't you ever heard of the little choo-choo that thought he could?"

They had heard of the little choo-choo that thought he could, but our car hadn't. A hundred yards up, the car decided to go no farther and we were stuck there with a bulky trailer that had to be backed down a narrow road. Unable to back a trailer even in a straight line on a wide road, I ended up unhitching the trailer and holding on desperately while it rolled downhill to the parking area. We did then walk up to the pueblo, and the ten days that followed heard many references to the little choo-choo that thought he could.

I learned a lesson that day about how hard it was to pull behind me a fully-loaded trailer. As long as the road was level and the way easy, that burden could be managed. But let the road get steep and the way hard, and that trailer had to be unhitched and removed, because its weight would quickly grind us to a halt.

In one of his most insightful sentences, Paul urged all of us to unhitch the trailer. Don't carry the unnecessary past around with you as a burden, or it will stop you. And here is how he said it: "One thing I do," he said. "Forgetting what lies behind and straining forward to what lies ahead, I press on toward the goal for the prize of the heavenly call of God in Jesus Christ" (Philippians 3:13-14).

Forgetting what lies behind. It may be a strange lesson for Memorial Day and, in a sense, it doesn't seem to be a very satisfactory suggestion, does it? A lot of us have tried to solve our problems by forgetting about them, and it never seems to work. The strange klunk the car keeps making doesn't get any better by forgetting it, nor does the mortgage on the house or the premium on the insurance.

It is through attention paid to such lessons from the past that we learn. Someone once asked a very successful man the secret of his success. "The secret of my success," the man said: "two words." "What are they?" he was asked. "Good decisions!" "But how can you make good decisions?" "One word," he said: "experience!" "Yes, but how can you get experience?" they asked. "Two words," he said: "bad decisions!"

The lessons of the past we keep with us, for, as the philosopher Santayana said, "Whoever does not learn from the past is doomed to repeat it." Lessons from the past we retain and use to guide our lives into something better. People from the past we retain, and we give thanks for them. This is the purpose of Memorial Day, to remember and give thanks for those people of the past whose influence and sacrifice have given us a country and a community and a church and a family.

Then if Paul was not thinking of this type of thing, what *was* he advising us to forget? He seemed to know from personal experience how burdensome the past could be if he carried too much of it around with him. To function effectively, to get up many difficult hills in life, it is necessary to unload from the trailer of the past those things which pull us back and grind us to a halt. And so Paul said, "Forgetting those things that lie behind," and we ask, "Forgetting *what* things that lie behind?" Paul's list would probably be identical to our own.

The trailer gets full of *disappointment with the way life has turned out,* for example, and this pulls us back and slows us down, and sometimes stops us completely. And Paul knew that disappointment well. After all, he was writing these words to the Philippians from prison, and no doubt, prison had not been in his original plans for himself.

Fifteen years of working for the gospel of Christ, fifteen years of traveling and preaching and enduring hardships, and what was there to show for it? Prison! Surely that was cause for disappointment, and was one of those things Paul *had to forget* in order to continue.

There are more than a few of us today who share the same need to forget our disappointment with how life has turned out. The job wasn't all it was cracked up to be. The children didn't graduate, the marriage didn't work out, the in-laws are a torment, the house was unwisely chosen— and the list goes on. At some point in life, nearly everyone lies awake in the middle of the night and wonders, in the words of the recently popular song, "Is *this* all there is?"

There is an essay written by the ancient Chinese scholar, Chin Shan-t'an, in which he wrote about the thirty-three happy moments of his life. Think of it: An entire lifetime remembered, and only thirty-three happy moments emerged. No wonder disappointment with life becomes a burden pulling us back. The worst kind of disappointment with life is grief, and many find that they cannot manage it. The vehicle of their life simply stops short. Disraili once put it this way: "Grief is the agony of an instant. The *indulgence of grief* is the blunder of a lifetime."

We find ourselves in a different kind of prison from the one Paul was in, but disappointment with life is a prison nonetheless. The only way to get out is to unload the trailer. Sometime ago, a television program which features unusual incidents showed a package that had been mailed to a prisoner in a federal penitentiary. The package had been returned to the sender by the U.S. Post Office and stamped on the package was a brief explanation of why the package had not been delivered. The stamped message said, "Escaped. Left no forwarding address." It's good advice. If you can unhitch the trailer, if you can escape from the prison of disappointment with life, *don't leave a forwarding address!* "Forgetting those disappointments that lie behind...I press on."

If disappointment with life often overloads the trailer, *so does resentment of others.* Paul knew this well. One after another of his letters refers to the fact that someone deserted him, someone unjustly opposed him, someone slandered him, someone let him down. He remembered his co-worker, Demas, and said, "Demas, in love with this present world, has deserted me" (2 Timothy 4:10). He remembered how Simon Peter, whom he called Cephas, had not dealt honestly with him, saying one thing in one place, another thing in another (Galatians 2:11-14). To Timothy, he wrote: "Alexander the coppersmith did me great harm....beware of him" (2 Timothy 4:14-15). "At my first defense," he said, "no one came to my support, but all deserted me" (2 Timothy 4:16).

Has anyone of us escaped this? Most of us have a list of our own. Whether we have lived on Main Street in the past or at the end of a country road, we have experienced some of this. Folks have not always been kind to us, or thoughtful, or fair. It doesn't take too good a memory to remember words that someone should never have said, had no right to say. It is tempting to collect these moments, to carry them around in our purse or billfold and get them out whenever the conversation pauses. They become, then, not stale memories from the past, dead and gone, but destructive forces in the present, wandering through our lives like some vicious animal loosed from its chains.

Our call is to unhitch the trailer of resentment and move on without it. Is it easy to do? No, it is one of the easiest things to preach and one of the hardest to practice. After all, look at Paul, giving us this excellent advice that leads us to life. "Forgetting what lies behind," he wrote, "I press on." And yet because Paul himself could not always practice what he preached, he wrote down his resentments at Demas and Alexander and all those who disappointed him. He didn't forget those resentments soon enough.

How long will *we* wait? That grudge we hold against someone, that bitterness toward a former friend, that resentment at an ungrateful daughter-in-law or acid-tongued mother-in-law: How long will we let it keep pulling back on our lives? "Forgetting those resentments that lie behind...I press on."

What about *our regrets at our own mistakes?* How loaded up is your life with *that* weighty burden? Paul had an unusual life, in that no one mapped it out for him. No boss or superior told him what to do or where to go. He was his own dispatcher, and every day, every moment, was a crossroads experience for him. Should he go over to Philippi for awhile now, or stay in Corinth? Was it time to move on to Rome, or beyond to Spain?

Surely Paul must have second-guessed himself from time to time. His visit to Athens turned out miserably, and Paul must have questioned his own judgment in going there. The church in Corinth stayed in a constant, unending quarrel, and Paul must have regretted his strategy there. Why did I go there? Why didn't I do this, or that?

It is always haunting for a person to wonder what his or her life would have been had a different turn been taken at some crossroads moment five years ago, or twenty or fifty. What if I had chosen a different college, taken a different job, moved to a different town, married a different spouse, had a different number of children? Sometimes we let our regrets almost stall us out. I knew a man who owned several hundred acres on what was, in the mid-1940s, the outskirts of Dallas. Immediately after the war, convinced that the boom times were over, he sold it for about one one-hundredth of what it would bring in the 1970s. We very seldom had a conversation without his mentioning his bad decision of 1945. His whole life was colored by regret.

Omar Khayyam's well-known verse says it for all of us:

The Moving Finger writes; and, having writ,
Moves on: nor all your Piety nor Wit
    Shall lure it back to cancel half a Line,
Nor all your Tears wash out a Word of it.[1]

It is past, over and done, and is best unhitched and
forgotten. "Forgetting these regrets that lie behind...I
press on."

Jesus Christ has promised us a life of fullness and joy.
To remember that promise means to forget our disappointment with life, our resentment of others, our regrets about
ourselves and "press on." Perhaps this anonymous poet
expressed it for us. The poem is called, simply, "For Sale."

> Some strong resentments which have ceased
>   to be of use to me,
> A stock of envy of the rich, some slightly
>   shopworn jealousy,
> A large supply of gloom that I shall have no
>   use for from today,
> I offer bargains—who will buy? Come bid,
>   and take the stuff away.
>
> A lot of wishes I've outgrown, a stock of
>   foolish old beliefs,
> Some pride I once was glad to own, a bulky
>   line of misfit grief.
> A large assortment of ill-will, a host of
>   sullenness and doubt,
> Harsh words that still have stingers on,
>   come on, come on, I'm closing out!
>
> I need more room for kindliness, for hopeful
>   courage and good cheer.
> For sale the hatred I possess, the dark
>   suspicions, and the fear.
> A large supply of frailties I shall have no use
>   for from today,
> I offer bargains, who will buy? Come bid and
>   take the stuff away!

Chances are you won't find a buyer for your disappointment, your resentments and regrets. But you can get rid of
them anyway. Unhitch the trailer. Let go of the useless
dead weight. "Forgetting what lies behind and straining
forward to what lies ahead, I press on toward the goal for
the prize of the heavenly call of God in Christ Jesus."

[1]Omar Khayyam, "The Rubaiyat," LXXI.

8 | *Independence Sunday*

Do You Have a Constitution?

Romans 13:1-8

Do you remember July 4, 1976? It seems but an instant ago for some of us. It was our nation's bicentennial, and it fell on a Sunday. Two hundred years earlier, the Declaration of Independence had been signed, and we were a free nation. Remember the celebrations? The great ships in the New York harbor, the exploding fireworks, the oratory? Our Declaration of Independence was two hundred years old.

Ten years after the Declaration of Independence, another event occurred of equal, or perhaps greater, importance. On September 17, 1786, after years of struggle and debate, the Constitution of the United States was signed and forwarded to the states for ratification. Two events of monumental significance, but which, in your estimation, was *more* important: the Declaration of Independence, or the Constitution?

I remember Labor Day weekend, 1948. My own personal Declaration of Independence was issued, if not signed. At age seventeen, after years of devoted service to the King and Queen at my house, the yoke of servitude became oppressive, and I declared Independence. I was off for college, finding there a freedom that was exhilarating and full. No checking when I came in at night, no reminder of homework, no tips about table manners or dress codes. That first week of complete freedom was a dizzying experience. Then reality set in, and I discovered that either I found some sort of discipline, or else I would be returned rather quickly to the dependence of home.

It is one thing to be independent, to be free, but some sort of order has to be imposed from without or from within, or that freedom becomes destructive anarchy.

So with our nation in 1776. Freedom was grand but it would be lost if some sort of order could not be voluntarily devised and accepted for the nation. So in that critical decade from 1776 to 1786, the free and independent nation sought a constitution.

Why did it take so long? Anyone who has sat on a committee trying to decide what color to paint a classroom ought to know. Fierce differences of opinion existed about almost every conceivable issue raised, and negotiations and compromise were necessary at every turn. Those decisions made more than two hundred years ago have given our nation its cast and character of today.

How should the states be represented in Congress: according to their population, or equally? A compromise was reached: The Senate could be apportioned with equal representation, the House according to population.

How should slaves be counted in the population? Illustrating the fact these decision makers were far from perfect, they decided that each slave should be counted as 4/5ths of a free person.

How should taxes be levied? Who should decide on disputes between states? Where did states' rights end and federal authority prevail? How strong an executive should there be? What role should legislative, executive, and judicial branches play in the enactment and enforcement of laws?

Again, freedom was heady and exhilarating, but unless the states could accept a constitution that voluntarily *limited freedom*, the new nation could not be born. And there were those who fiercely resisted the new Constitution, and opposed any federal restriction of freedom.

Remember Patrick Henry? It was Patrick Henry's fiery words that had led to the Declaration of Independence. Who can ever forget those words spoken in May of 1776? "Is life so dear or peace so sweet as to be purchased at the price of chains, of slavery? Forbid it, Almighty God. I know not what course others may take, but as for me, give me liberty or give me death!"

Patrick Henry was great at rebellion or revolution, but after the was was over and the United States were struggling for order, for a constitution, Patrick Henry kept right on rebelling. He refused to attend most of the Constitutional Convention, and when the Virginia legislators considered ratification of the Constitution in 1788, Patrick Henry's fiery oratory rang out against it to the bitter end. He objected, for example, to the way it began, "We the people of the United States," because the people never got to vote on it, only the state legislatures. So his suggestion was that the preamble should begin with "We the States," not "We the people."

Finally, after long and intense struggle in the legislatures of each of the thirteen states, the Constitution was formally ratified in June, 1788. What an incredibly creative and significant document the Constitution was and is. For the first time in world history, a harness had been devised for democracy that made it workable. It was not perfect, of course, but it included devices for careful and ordered change.

No political system, no form of government, can ever substitute for the integrity of its citizens. But the Constitution, now over two centuries old, gave us a way to make democracy stable and workable. That is what we also celebrate and thank God for, this weekend.

Again, it should be stated clearly. Freedom is magnificent, but order and discipline have to be imposed from within or, without it, that sparkling freedom turns sour and produces nothing. This principle applies to each of us in our own personal lives. Many a person who has, in a moment of courage, declared independence from some tyranny and gained freedom has never devised a constitution by which to order his or her life, and that freedom has gone bad.

Young single persons experience this struggle more than most others. Once school is over, a job received, obligations minimized, debts paid, a pretty good salary coming in, we experience a period of freedom we haven't

ever known before and probably won't ever know again.
There is no warden closing the gates and ringing the bell.
We don't have to keep declaring our independence in this
period; it is there, for all to see.

But many find that a glut of freedom doesn't bring the
rewards they thought it would, and the order that some
impose on themselves, the obligations they freely accept—
the chains, if you will, that they wear—seem to bring them
more joy than does boundless independence. Only when
their declarations of independence give way to some voluntarily accepted constitution or order does meaning come.

Often we emphasize our freedom in matters of religion
more than our responsibilities and obligations. We declare
independence in religion, but we stop short of devising a
religious constitution for ourselves, setting forth what we
want to be free *for*.

It is easier to devise declarations of independence of
religion than constitutions. The old evangelical question,
"Brother, sister, are you *saved*?" The emphasis is usually
on what we are saved *from*—we are saved from guilt, from
sin, from death, from eternal damnation. Get saved, and
you are free from all these things. But saved for what?

At home we sometimes say, "Are we going to save this
or that article? Yes? Then put it in the attic if we want to
save it." Some would see the church as a sort of religious
attic into which saved persons are put. But this is obviously
incomplete. Saved for what? What do we intend to *do* with
our freedom from guilt and sin? To be born again means to
be born to a life of integrity and responsibility and righteousness, and most persons need some sort of personally
ratified constitution which guides them in turning religious
freedom into responsible living.

Each one of us has devised some sort of religious
constitution, whether it is written or not, consciously
identified or not.

• Does my unwritten religious constitution say anything about how often I worship God?

• Does my constitution count people of other races as 4/
5ths of a person, or as whole people?

• Does my constitution ever direct me to the aching
needs of hungry and hurting people around the world, or
does it keep me focused only on my own needs?

• Does my constitution point me in any way to people in this world whose struggle for freedom continues, or does it direct my gaze to what I have attained?

•Does my constitution say anything about gossip and slander and fault finding? Does it cover how much of my income I give away? Does it deal with clean language or honesty or decency?

You see why many a person who declares independence in religion never creates a constitution. No wonder that religion remains unsatisfying to many: They never give it order and structure, so it can have no strength. In this sense, then, constitutions are more important than declarations of independence, and unless you have one for your life and until you get one, this freedom you enjoy will be lacking something.

John Killinger writes about a lovely young woman who came to his office with a baby in her arms and a slightly older child pulling at her dress and acting up. Killinger says: "She had only a few minutes to talk because she was picking up her third child from the preschool when she left. She apologized for her hair which she had not had time to comb properly for that morning, and for her dress which had been clean when she left home but now showed traces of milk and juice and a shade or two of baby food. We had already discussed what she came to see me about and she was readjusting one child on her hip, pacifying the other, picking up scattered toys from the floor. 'Wow!' she said. 'When I think that five years ago I was dying to get married and move out of my parents' house in order to be free, it almost blows my mind!'"[1] And yet, it was in her gladly accepted chains that she found freedom's meaning, fulfillment, and joy.

Back, then, to our nation. The Constitution is, in a sense, the Dr. Spock for raising justice and freedom. But justice and freedom are messy babies. They spit up on us and they cry all night. But they are worth raising.

Thank God, then, for freedom and for those patriots who brought it to us. But thank God even more for our kind of constitution, national or personal, that takes freedom and puts it to work in responsibility.

[1]*Pulpit Digest,* July, 1987, p. 299.

9 | *Labor Sunday*

The Illusion of Excellence

Philippians 1:1-11

Consider this very timely question as September once again rolls around: What kind of goals should our team have for the upcoming football season? There have been some good seasons and some bad in the past but a new season is about to begin. What kind of goals should we have?

Suppose the coach announces to all that his goal is the championship. Suppose we win eight and lose three and just miss the play-offs. Much better than last year, but the goal was not reached. Would that be cause for despair?

Or suppose he reminds us that this is a rebuilding year, and says that the goal is four victories, and in December we exactly reach that goal. Would that be occasion for great rejoicing?

Our question is, is it better to set low goals and reach them, or set high goals and risk not quite making it?

It is a stubbornly persistent question, and faces us in every area of life. As a parent, how do you help teenagers set goals? Do you advise easy goals that do not test the youth, or high goals that may subject him or her to disappointment? How does a preacher address a congregation in setting a budget for a new year? Easy goals that give everyone a sense of accomplishment? Or tough goals that stretch us, cause us to grow, and yet might not be reached?

Paul faced that in writing to his friends in Philippi. He knew how hard a battle they faced. They were a new religion in a corrupt town. A minority, an unimportant powerless minority. Wouldn't he have been justified in suggesting easy goals for them? Knowing full well the reality of the situation, Paul's advice was unequivocal. As J. B. Phillips translates the passage, Paul said to them, "I want you to be able always to recognize the highest and the best" (Philippians 1:10). Paul's advice about goal setting? The highest and the best!

But back from Philippi to our town and to us. What kind of goals do we set for ourselves? In our own personal lives what kind of target do we aim toward? When I face this question in my own life, I am helped greatly by recognizing three facts about life itself. See if they help you in your own task of goal setting.

First, let us recognize the attraction of easy goals. Believing myself to be getting a little out of shape, I decide to take up jogging. My goal is to jog out to the end of the driveway every morning to pick up the paper, and then, after a short rest, to jog back. Seeing pudginess as a part of my problem, I resolve that between now and Christmas, I will lose one pound. I am standing in the need of prayer, so my goal is that I will say grace before at least one meal a week. Feeling the need for Bible study, I resolve that sometime within the next two weeks I will read John 3:16.

Easy goals! Now these may be exaggerations, but they symbolize what we do all the time. It would have been easy for Paul to do this for his friends at Philippi. "Listen," he might have said, "I know your situation, so I don't expect too much from you. A few of us who had personal experiences with Jesus, we have high obligations. But I can't expect too much of you. So just hang in there. If you can't be too good, at least don't be too bad. I want you to aim toward being *moderately good and fairly decent.*"

There is something appealing about easy goals. They seduce us quickly. Why do people respond to those incredible ads in the newspaper that say, "Eat all you want, and still lose weight"? Should we reach for the best? That's too hard.

The moderately good and the fairly decent: That's just the ticket for me!

So we yield to easy goals, struggling feverishly toward four and seven seasons, aiming toward mediocrity and achieving it, and gaining a small amount of satisfaction with being moderately good and fairly decent. For sadly, in this world we live in, being moderately good and fairly decent stands out. It's a long way from reaching for the best, but it's better than most. Who was it that said it first: "In the kingdom of the blind, the one-eyed man is king."

The attraction of easy goals. Listen, you young people, you need to watch this especially. Don't learn this lesson from us grown-ups. Don't be satisfied with mediocrity just because we often seem to be. Jessie Rittenhouse's poem advises us well:

> I bargained with Life for a penny,
>   And Life would pay no more.
> However, I begged at evening,
>   When I counted my scanty store.
>
> For Life is a just employer,
>   She gives you what you ask.
> But once you have set the wages,
>   You're left with your chosen task.
>
> I worked for a servant's hire,
>   Only to learn, dismayed,
> That any wage I had asked of Life,
>   Life would have gladly paid.[1]

When I think of targets for my own life, I remember frequently the attraction of easy goals.

There is a second warning thought in the setting of goals: *the illusion of apparent excellence.* The illusion of *apparent* excellence. And I tell you with all the force I can muster, that this is a trademark of much of our American culture today. If we cannot, if we *will not*, reach for the best, we can at least pretend to be there. Try on for size these two curious examples of the kind of thing we do today in creating the "illusion of apparent excellence."

Have you ever seen a Bradley G-T driving down the street? The most popular model has an old Rolls-Royce appearance—an open touring-car body, chrome plated, exposed piping, low, sleek. It looks as though it ought to be driven by an Aristotle Onassis or a Prince Ranier. I first saw it displayed in airport lobbies several years ago. Wouldn't it be fun to drive *that* up to a party at a friend's house, or into the minister's parking place at church?

Here's what it is. The Bradley G-T Company manufactures fiberglass car bodies, complete with chrome piping and all the fancies. You buy a Volkswagen bug of almost any vintage, remove the VW body from the chassis, lower the beautiful fiberglass body onto it, make all the proper connections, and suddenly as you drive down main street all heads are turning in your direction. You've got something that may not be the best but it sure looks like it! People think you're driving a $75,000 sports car, and only you know that it is nothing more than a VW Beetle with a wig on.

Or here's one advertised in *Saturday Review*. It's for those who serve a glass of wine occasionally to their guests. If the bottle you serve from looks as if it has come only this afternoon from Safeway, it loses some of its allure. But if it looks as if it has just been carefully brought up from some deep wine cellar, it naturally tastes better.

Therefore, Gordon Bennett & Associates, Inc., manufactures and sells phony wine-bottle dust. Before your guests arrive, sprinkle the dust liberally over the unopened bottle and then, at the proper time, bring out the bottle of wine "besprinkled with the dust of centuries." It may not be the best, but it looks it!

These are ridiculous, but real, examples, and they hint at what may well be a growing inner weakness of our nation today—this willingness to accept the *illusion of excellence* without its reality.

This is Labor Sunday, and nowhere more clearly than in our work does this national malaise show up. Our labor is the basic fiber of our nation and it was once founded on excellence. It was founded on hard work, sacrifice, sweat, and tears. Behind the facade of our nation was the reality of quality in what we did, in our reach for the best of labor, technology, industry. In all the world, there was no need for illusion. It *was* the best. But now, in so many fields, we settle for the *illusion* of apparent excellence.

In the field of education, for example, a debate now centers on the question of whether students have a right to receive a high-school diploma without doing the work to earn it. The phrase the educators use to define the question is "entitlement without qualification." Are students *entitled* to a high-school diploma without being qualified for it? The illusion of apparent excellence comes as we are *declaring* people to be educated when they, in fact, are not. To claim excellence without creating it is vain!

But we see it in other fields as well. In labor, where we demand high wages without hard work. In the professions, where we receive great honor and out-of-balance income without demonstrating a balancing personal responsibility to go with it. In the military, where we often have power without true patriotism. In politics, where we have influence without integrity.

This is the malaise in American life today, and on this Labor Sunday it stands out clearly—the illusion of apparent excellence.

There remains only the need to state it positively, this idea we have been entertaining. Yes, we recognize the attraction of easy goals. Yes, we see the illusion of apparent excellence. But put positively, it is simply this: *There is power in high goals.* There is a dynamic power in setting the highest and the best as our goal, for the very act of reaching for genuine excellence strengthens us, and remakes us beyond our expectation. We tend to become what we aim at!

It bears repeating. *We tend to become what we aim at.* It's true in so very many ways. You young people making plans for your lives: Aim low and you'll likely hit low. Aim high and that's likely where you'll end. When you choose a goal, you determine a destination.

In marriage: If the goal is a life of shared joy, lived together, then the very act of reaching for that will enrich your lives, and you will be the chief benefactors of your own high goals. But if the goal is simply to make do, if the goal in marriage is enduring mediocrity, then you will be sentenced to sharing the misery of that achievement.

In church programs: What do we want our church to be? What kind of enthusiasm and joy in giving and serving and worshiping might we wish to discover? We will become whatever we aim at.

We are putting our finger here on the very essence of religion. God is true excellence, the highest and the best, drawing us up out of our lesser selves. Jesus Christ is the highest and the best example of what human life can be like. This is why we come to worship. It is our reach for the best, drawing us up, making us leave our patios and breakfast tables and newspapers, drawing us to worship.

The act of worship is an act of responding to genuine excellence. I am convinced that the French theologian, Teilhard de Chardin, was right. From the dawn of time, humanity has been moving upward, drawn by the magnetic power of God, pulled upward by the lure of excellence, drawn out of the primordial slime, out of the swamps, out of primitive chaos. We are being pulled along by God's goodness, drawn upward by Jesus Christ—upward toward the stars of a fulfillment that God will bestow upon us in God's good time.

And every offering of the best that WE make, everything that is good and beautiful, everything that is rich in authentic excellence—music that soars and poetry that inspires, radiant windows that shimmer with light, experiences in worship that stir us, profound literature and deep prayer, great acts of heroism and little acts of courage, love offered freely and received joyfully, little children singing and older folk praying and giving, and so much more—all are examples of reaching for the best, lifting us regularly out of little swamps of despair and into the presence of God.

The contest will go on as long as we live, as we are pulled between the highest and lowest, best and worst—genuine excellence and its deceptive illusions. It is in our setting of personal goals that we decide how the contest will be played out. And since, in every area of life, we tend to become just what we reach for, I urge upon you with every ounce of persuasiveness I can muster: In every moment of choosing, don't settle for an illusion of excellence. Make your goal the highest and the best!

[1]Jessie Rittenhouse, "My Wage."

10 | *Election Sunday*

Electing
a Leader

Galatians 6:7-10

Forty-eight hours from now, when I step into the voting booth and cast my vote for the presidency of the United States, I am going to be carrying something dangerous with me. I wonder if you'll be carrying it with you, too. Millions of Americans will, I am sure.

What I'm going to be carrying with me is the plaintive expectation that my choice for president will solve all this nation's problems. That if my candidate just wins, then everything will be fine, nothing more will be required of me, and we will all be able to start leaning back and living happily ever after.

It's an old desire, and it makes me think of a warning given by the transplanted Missouri poet, T. S. Eliot: "Beware of dreaming of systems so perfect that no one has to be good." Do you catch the danger in that? "Beware of dreaming of systems so perfect—or churches so perfect, or presidents so perfect, or military power so perfect, or laws so perfect—that no one has to be good."

But I'll be carrying it with me this Tuesday, even though I will make the effort to leave it at home—this unrealistic wish that we could find ourselves a leader who will absolve each of us individually of the hard, ongoing responsibilities of daily integrity and citizenship, a leader who can wave some Washington wand and make the troubles of the world go away.

Do you believe that this is an old problem? Let me show you. Go back three thousand years to the time of the Judges in the Old Testament. It was 1050 B.C., and the people of Israel were living in a chaotic time. The very last verse of the book of Judges describes that time in a phrase that seems to leap across these thirty centuries to depict us too. It reads: "In those days there was no king in Israel; all the people did what was right *in their own eyes*" (Judges 21:25).

To find a solution to this chaotic anarchy, a committee was organized. They studied the situation, and they came up with a solution. *If* the right man could be found, *if* they had a king like all the other nations, then all this chaos would go away and their problems would be solved. So a king was chosen. The old prophet Samuel nominated the candidate, a man named Saul, and in a great ceremony at Mizpah Saul was acclaimed king by the people.

And now, at last, they had what they wanted, and the future looked promising for Israel. They were enthusiastic about their new leader. Surely, he would solve the problem of the ever-present threat of war with the Philistines; surely he would improve the internal wranglings that went on; surely the economic problems would be given solution. They believed it heartily! A new day was dawning for them. They had themselves a king so perfect that no one would have to be good, or honest, or energetic, or patriotic. Happy days were here again!

But alas, it was not to be. Foreign policy got worse, and the hated Philistines grew stronger and more threatening. The domestic situation deteriorated, and internal corruption increased and Israel tottered on the very brink of annihilation.

It was the usual situation. Even after the leader had been elected, not much improvement could be seen in the nation, because not much improvement could be seen in the people! Bitter was the disappointment of many. So great had been their expectations at the time of the election, so few had been the accomplishments afterward. Why? It was not really the fault of King Saul; he had led quite ably. The fault was that the people had carried something into their voting booth that was and is dangerous. They had looked for something in their system of government that it simply could not give to them, nor can any system give it.

Look back there when the Israelites first asked Samuel for a king, and listen to what the people had said. "No!" they insisted, "but we are determined to have a king over us, so that we also may be like other nations, and that our king may govern us and go out before us and fight our battles" (1 Samuel 8:19-20). Take note of that: *that he may fight our battles!* No wonder the people of Israel were disappointed, just as are folk throughout the centuries—including this present one—who seek to make their government and their leaders responsible for fighting the battles in which all of us must participate.

The real battles of life are not fought by proxy in this way. The king could never do for the people what the people had to do for themselves. When *we* face an election as we are now doing, this is *our* temptation too, this pretension that the leaders we choose will be able to go out for us and fight our battles. They will represent us, to be sure. They will affect our thinking, of course, and the careful selection process we face on Tuesday is important. But the real health of this nation depends on our own integrity, on our own individual willingness to get into the battle for decency and righteousness in our nation.

Professor William Muehl of Yale Divinity School tells of visiting a fine old ancestral home in Connecticut. The aged owner, ninety years old, was giving him a guided tour of the old house. "As we stood in the main room talking," he said, "I noticed an old rifle hanging over the fireplace. I was struck by its beauty and wanted to take it down and examine it more closely. But as I reached out, the old woman quickly caught my arm and said, 'Please don't touch it. It's loaded and might go off.' When I raised an inquiring eyebrow, she went on to say, 'My great-great-great-grandfather loaded that gun and put it there against the day when he might stroke a blow for the freedom of the American colonies.' I drew what I still feel was the logical inference from the situation and asked,'Then the old gentleman died before the Revolution?' 'No,' my hostess responded, 'he lived to a ripe old age and died in 1817, but he just never seemed able to generate much enthusiasm for General Washington's rebellion.'"[1]

Now fortunately, many early Americans didn't feel that way, and enough got into the battle to secure independence for this country. In similar fashion today, the battle for our nation's integrity does not depend so much on the individual who leads it as much as it does on the people who make it up. I do believe that the morality of a nation begins with the people and works up to its leadership, rather than the other way around. The spirit and commitment of the people will determine the level of the nation itself. Water cannot rise higher than its source, we are told, and neither can national morality.

In this period of national decision, each one of us has an opportunity to think about his or her own role in this nation's life. A reporter once covered a campaign rally back in the mountains of Kentucky, and watched as the politicians made their speeches, to the loud yells of the mountain people. When one finished, the reporter asked a fellow who had taken a leading role in the cheering: "What did you think about the speech you just heard?" Back quickly came the reply: "I didn't come here to think. I came here to holler!"

Just occasionally during the next two days, we need to stop hollering and start thinking—thinking, perhaps, about William Penn's statement made two centuries ago: "Governments, like clocks, go from the motion men give them; governments, then, depend upon men more than men upon governments. Let men be good and the government cannot be bad; but if men be bad, let the government be ever so good, they will warp and spoil it to their own turn."

William Penn's observation puts the pressure on us, in our daily lives—and by implication, I think, tells us that even more important than how we vote next Tuesday is how we determine to live for the next four years.

• As long as families live in big or little immorality, then the nation will find immorality a common thing on all levels of life.

• As long as we in our everyday language use racial terms that wound and injure people of other races, there is going to be racial strife on a national scale.

• As long as there is petty dishonesty on the part of the

common citizen—whether in income tax returns, or family business, or whatever—there will be grand dishonesty too.

• As long as there is a cynicism on the part of the people, a feeling that every one of us should get what we can when we can and however we can, then this attitude will be found on higher levels too.

The ancient alchemists used to dream of making gold by rearranging the makeup of baser metals. Some dream today that righteous nations can be produced by rearranging unrighteous people—that there must be a governmental system so good that it, alone, will produce justice and righteousness. But we should be clear on this point. Unrighteous people create an unrighteous nation, whatever its form or whoever its leader might be. Righteous people acting in concert create a righteous nation, whatever its form or whoever its leader might be.

"Give us a king who will go out before us and fight our battles." When the people of Israel chose a king, they felt that, by the selection of a leader, they absolved themselves of their own responsibilities of fighting those battles. So the problems continued to exist in the nation, because the problems continued to exist in the hearts of the people. And that's a battleground where no king or president can ever fight.

A city mayor in France once organized a great wine festival for his city. Each winemaker in the county was asked to bring one gallon of his best wine and pour it into a large barrel in the center of the city square. The collected wine would become the chief refreshment during the ensuing celebration.

One after another the growers came and poured their gallon of wine into the great container. When all had finished, the mayor drew the first glass. Before all the assembled people, he tasted it. Imagine their surprise when he sputtered and angrily threw the contents to the ground. Each of the growers, it turned out, had thought that his own small contribution was not important, and had brought water instead of wine—so that the whole barrel was filled with nothing but sweetened water.

The spirit, the flavor, of a nation or of a church is the sum total of what each one of us contributes to it. If we have genuine concern about our nation, the best thing we can do for it is to begin where we are, give our lives here and now to Jesus Christ, pledge ourselves to personal integrity and decency and compassion. Any one of us may think that our own individual contribution is lost amid the multitudes of others. But that is not so.

This sermon has but one point: to emphasize the importance of your own family's integrity and righteousness in the effort to strengthen our nation, to say that the best way for you to strengthen your nation is to be a decent, honest, compassionate citizen here and now. Perhaps this poem sums it up:

> Thy will be done on earth,
>   on bended knees we pray,
> Then leave our prayer before the throne
>   and rise,and go our way.
> And earth is filled with woe and war
>   and trouble still
> For lack of those whose prayer is, "Lord,
>   I've come to do thy will."
> "Thy will be done on earth?"
>   Lord, grant us grace to see
> That if thy will is to be done,
>   it must be done by me.

[1]William Muehl, *All the Damned Angels.* Pilgrim Press, 1972, p. 52.

11 | *Thanksgiving Sunday*

One of Our Very Best Words

Luke 17:11-19

How much is a word worth? Back when Rudyard Kipling was England's most popular writer, the news got out that his publishers paid him a dollar a word for his work. Some Cambridge students, hearing of this, cabled Kipling one dollar, along with instructions: "Please send us one of your very best words." Kipling replied with a one-word telegram: "Thanks."

This much is true: That word "thanks" *is*, indeed, one of our very best words—worth much to the person who speaks it and to the person who hears it. The writer of Proverbs expressed it succinctly: "A word fitly spoken is like apples of gold in a setting of silver" (Proverbs 25:11). "Thanks" is indeed a fitly spoken word.

Why, then, do we not speak it and hear it more often than we do? It is not because we are not grateful. We remember well the story of the ten lepers, in Luke 17. All of them were healed of their disease, but only one of them returned to say, "thank you" to Jesus. Sometimes that story is interpreted to mean that only one of them was grateful, but undoubtedly all of them were. The difference was that nine of them hurried home first, so as to greet their friends and attend to their business as soon as possible, intending, perhaps, to go back to Jesus soon afterward and thank him. But things turned out other than they had expected. They were kept at home longer than they meant to be, and in the meantime Jesus was gone. Only one of them had a disposition that made him act in time to say "thank you."

There is little doubt that we, today, are grateful for the immense blessings that we have received. But the Thanksgiving season is a time for giving explicit voice to our gratitude. And how vast is the list of those to whom we owe that simple but "very best" word.

"Thanks," to begin with, for our country. Undoubtedly we are appreciative of our country though we seldom put it into words. Our proper instinct for self-criticism sometimes blinds us to what we do right in this country, and we neglect expressions of thanksgiving.

To whom do we say "thanks" for our country? To people, patriots, long since dead. To pioneers who displayed more courage, more endurance of hardship in a week than some of us do in a lifetime. There's a place off the highway a few miles west of Kansas City where a marker points out the old wagon tracks made by the people who first went westward. Stand there, imagine their hopes and dreams, their fears and adversities, and say "thanks" for this country of ours.

We would say "thanks," as well, to all those people who have places in our lives that make our lives richer and more meaningful. Thanks to our families: our parents with their sacrifice, our children with their patience, our husbands and wives with their love and faithfulness. Thanks to friends whose trust and laughter set a light in life that gives us both warmth and sight.

Thanks to people in public service: politicians, governors, senators, presidents—people who endure unending criticism and receive little thanks. Thanks to teachers and administrators in our schools. Thanks to them for putting up with difficult children and unreasonable parents.

Thanks to nurses and doctors and custodians in hospitals. In every moment of need, day or night, they are always there. Thanks to safety officers who, in good weather and in bad, help little children across dangerous streets. Thanks to public utility people who are called out in storms and at all hours to keep our sources of power flowing. Thanks to those who are working right now in generating plants to give us power.

Thanks to police officers and fire fighters. We relax from our work occasionally but they are always on call. They deal with all the tragedies of life, and with some of our worst citizens. They deserve our thanks.

Thanks to truck drivers who keep our stores supplied with food. Thanks to butchers and bakers, and newspaper carriers and garbage collectors.

All these people as well as so many others constitute the spokes of the wheels on which our lives turn. We need them, and to them we say one of our very best words: "Thanks."

Should we not also say "thanks" for things—for the items and goods that enrich our lives? When I go home from church today I am going to be well fed. I have the good fortune of never having gone really hungry for a single day in my life, so I say "thanks" for food.

Thanks for good water to drink. Eddie Rickenbacker was once asked what was the biggest lesson he learned from drifting about with his companions in life rafts for twenty-one days on the Pacific Ocean. "The biggest lesson I learned," he said, "was that if you have all the fresh water you want to drink and all the food you need to eat, you ought never complain about anything." Thanks, for food and water.

Thanks for clothes to wear, for medicine which relieves pain and brings healing. Thanks, too, for luxuries that enhance life—for television and radio, for air conditioning and automatic furnaces, for telephones and refrigerators and good streets.

Thanks for knowing that seasons eventually end for losing teams, and new ones begin again. Thanks for an endless stream of new days and new opportunities for beginning again.

And thanks for the church. Thanks for the building, this place of quiet beauty given to us by a past generation. Thanks to those who do the work of the church—who today in the steaming jungles of Zaire, in dangerous Thailand, in the isolated plains of Nigeria, are living out and sharing the gospel in our name.

Thanks to those here who keep the work of the church going—who prepare the communion emblems on Saturdays, who lead the Scout troop, who sponsor our youth groups and teach Sunday school classes. Thanks to the deacons and ushers and elders, to those who make calls on new people in this community. Thanks to choir members who give an evening and a morning every week for the glory of God.

Thanks to those who are faithful to the church, who can be counted on to be here in worship on Sunday. Thanks to those who give generously to the church, who give gifts worthy of what they have. Thanks for the church and those who make it up.

The list is still incomplete. But there is another question that begs to be asked: *How best do we express our thanks for all of this?* Surely not by a tip of the hat, or a binge of eating on Thursday of this week.

We say "thank you" by committing ourselves to the best use of the bounty God has given us. How do you say "thank you" for a person who loves you and shares life with you? By commitment, isn't it? Utter commitment, without reservation. Singer Glen Campbell had a fascinating song a few years back that rose to number one on the charts by asserting in a fetching way that romantic love can survive only in the *absence* of permanent commitment. The song was called "Gentle on My Mind," and the singer explained that the reason he loved his girlfriend so much was that he knew he was not bound to her by any promises—he had not signed his name on any dotted line.

Do you see that? I love you so much and am so thankful for you because I don't have to commit anything to you. I can abandon you at any moment. I am not committed, nor obligated—and that's why I love you so much and am so thankful.

Now I enjoy Glen Campbell's music immensely, but I would debate the sentiments expressed here all the way. Do we convey gratitude for love by refusing to commit ourselves? No. We express gratitude by commitment.

We express gratitude for our country not by reserving the right to desert it when it needs us but by being willing to invest our best selves, our best thought, in it. We express gratitude for the church not by reserving the right to check out the first time it asks something of us—but by commitment. One of our best words, the word most fitly spoken, is "thanks"—and one of our best actions is commitment that arises out of gratitude.

Finally, let's go that one remaining step and say "thanks" most of all to God, for the gift of Jesus Christ, who gives meaning to life now and life eternal to come. Thanks to God for our knowing that nothing can ever happen to us that would take us away from God's loving care.

This is the glory of Thanksgiving. It lets gratitude bubble up to the surface, and, as we drink from it, something of the radiance of life is recaptured. How much we have!

The secret of the thankful life is to put that radiance, that blessedness, into words. One of our very best words is "thanks," and one of our very best actions is "giving." Put the two together and it *is* Thanksgiving!

Then what we are after is not just being blessed but feeling it, knowing it, responding to it, expressing it— coming to God and saying, "Lord, all this, so much, so much. How can I ever say 'thank you' for it?"

The answer comes back quickly. Are you thankful? Really thankful? Then let thanksgiving be lived. Let your gratitude find form, give it hands and feet. Give it voice and sound and sight. And put into action one of our very best words.

12 | Peace Sunday

Peace Breaks Out

Luke 2:8-14

Just think of it! Centuries from now, historians may be studying the events of the summer and fall of 1989 and saying, "That was the time it all began! That was the year when peace broke out. Wouldn't it have been wonderful to have been alive in those days?"

Do you suppose any of us suspect or realize what we are living through? At Advent time we recite the angel's song, "Glory to God in the highest heaven, and on earth peace among those whom he favors!" (Luke 2:14). From the beginning, the coming of Christ into the world and the celebration of Hanukkah have been linked with peace. Could it be, at last, that it is actually happening? There is a strange stirring in the trees, a whisper of hope abroad of late. Could it actually be? Is peace breaking out?

What an astounding variety of pictures we have recently been seeing. A telephone call comes from our son Steve, just winding up a five-week business assignment in Germany. On Thanksgiving weekend he went with a friend to Berlin and, in an amazing moment, visited the Wall. There was the symbol of a startling event: peace breaking out, peace represented by yawning gaps in the Wall, and clasped hands and dancing and candlelight and song. Who would have believed what they saw?

The events continue to tumble upon us with lightning speed, one after another. Someone once said that trying to determine what is going on in the world by reading the newspapers is like trying to tell the time by watching the second hand of a clock. They move so fast, these events, and we can scarcely believe what we are seeing. Consider:

• In the central square in Prague, Czechoslovakia, the square where Russian tanks rumbled twenty years earlier, there were one hundred thousand people waving flags, joining hands, dancing, calling for freedom.

• In East Germany, the churches were filled with tens of thousands of Germans, the cry going up, "End this senseless hostility and division," and raising up the great hymns of Martin Luther.

• In Rome, President Gorbachev and Pope John Paul II conferred and clasped hands and announced that freedom of religion would be reestablished in the USSR and the Roman Catholic Church would be restored to freedom in the Ukraine.

• Off Malta, the leaders of the two superpowers dialogued and debated, reached accords and signed agreements, made plans for future talks about arms reductions—and peace rode high over the choppy seas.

• From Kennedy Center in our nation's capitol, a televised program featured the combined voices of the U.S. Naval Academy Chorus and the Red Army Choir singing "God Bless America"!

What is all this? Has the world suddenly gone wonderfully crazy? In our day, in our time, can the angels' song actually be coming true—on earth, peace, good will among all people? Is peace breaking out?

God knows this is a need we've all felt, even here in our country that has escaped the worst ravages of war in this century. The third verse of the Christmas hymn, "It Came upon a Midnight Clear," is not sung very often, but it expresses our deepest feelings vividly:

> Yet with the woes of sin and strife,
>   The world has suffered long,
> Beneath the angel strain have rolled
>   Two thousand years of wrong;

And man, at war with man, hears not
  The love song which they bring:
O hush the noise, ye men of strife,
  And hear the angels sing!

Two thousand years of strife and slaughter and massacre, and all of us know the illogical awfulness of war. We ought to, right here in Kansas City, for just ten blocks down our street one can still hear distant echoes of an ugly battle fought one hundred and twenty five years ago, the Battle of Westport. Walk through the peacefulness of Loose Park and see if you can hear the sound of cannon roaring, catch the muskets' flash, the bayonets red with the blood of boys—always boys—until finally, mercifully, peace broke out in this fractured nation of ours.

If you have read Kurt Vonnegut's novel, *Slaughterhouse Five,* you may remember the scene which shows American bombers attacking a German city, fiercely repelled by German defenses. Somehow the film of time starts running backwards, the scenes grow strange. German cities are engulfed in flaming fire storms, but the flames suddenly go out, and the cities stand intact, peaceful. And the bombs go rising back up from the city, back into the bombers. The jagged shrapnel comes out of the wounded bodies of American flyers, back into the explosive anti-aircraft shells which are drawn back into the guns below. And the bombers fly backwards to Britain. The young crews emerge healthy and safe. The bombs go back to America where they disassemble themselves and their materials are buried back in the earth, and the boys come back to the scattered towns from which they started, and they walk with the girls on a thousand Main Streets back home.

Every war could be run backwards like that, so that we could see what might have been. Every war seems necessary when it breaks out, and senseless when it is over. We know, in retrospect, the illogical waste and tragedy of war. That's why what we are seeing coming timidly forward in this world of ours seems so strange. Could it really be? Is peace breaking out? Are the angels singing again?

So how do we respond to all of this? How have you been feeling, as you have watched recent events unfold on TV and read about "peace dividends" and global realignments and the head of the "evil empire" being invited to sit in on a NATO meeting?

Some react with a measure of cynicism. Asked how he felt about the promising developments in the world, Senator Phil Gramm responded, "It may well be that we are about to enter that biblical era when the lion and the lamb can lie down together. I will feel safer, however, if we are the lion."

And that is precisely why peace is so elusive. Even in peace, we want to be the lion. So used are we to tension and turmoil that, while we may yearn for peace and pray for it, we don't really trust it when it is actually threatening to come through the front door.

There *is* something comfortable about keeping barriers up between us and the other folk, and so we react to this real and symbolic dismantling of the wall between East and West with caution. Are we moving too fast? What is the catch here, the hidden agenda? We are somewhat like the dog that chases cats. Around the house and down the street they go, until by some fortuitous turn of chance the dog corners the cat. And what does he do next? As often as not, he sits down and scratches, or remembers a previous engagement and off he lopes. Cats are good for chasing. Catching them is another matter altogether.

Is peace like that? Are we always to remain impulsive in war and cautious in peace? Shouldn't it be just the opposite? John Foster Dulles once said, "The world will never have lasting peace so long as people reserve for war the finest human qualities: sacrifice, courage, loyalty, devotion. Peace, no less than war, requires our finest gifts." Peace requires courage, sacrifice, valor. While we will pay that price for war, we are afraid to risk it for peace.

So the question for us may be, will we *let* peace break out? What happens if God at last sends out the dove of peace and it has no place among us to land? Will it be, could it be, that decades from now those historians will look back sadly on this time and ponder, "That was our chance! Just think, the door to peace was cracked open, and we could have walked through it! Oh, that we had that opportunity again!"

How, then, can we claim the gift of peace when it is offered to us? Real peace is not cheap, because it is more than just the absence of war. The Hebrew word for peace, "shalom," means the condition where justice and righteousness exist for all, not just for a favored few. The Chinese word for peace, I am told, is made up of three symbols joined together. The three symbols stand for "rice in the mouth," "roof over family," and "two hearts parallel." That's what peace must be built upon, across this world: food to eat, homes to live in, and cordiality and respect.

Thus the uncomfortable fact for us in this country is that we cannot live insulated from and unconcerned about injustices that exist around the world. *Real* peace is a *by-product* of justice and righteousness, which is precisely what Christ calls us to create for this world. We may sign accords with the USSR and China, and the European nations may opt for freedom and democracy, but the greatest threat to peace will then come from a dozen corners on the globe where injustice flourishes.

As long as the Palestinians in Gaza and the West Bank have no homes, as long as blacks in South Africa have no justice, as long as peasants in Central America have little opportunity, as long as students in China have no freedom, peace will remain elusive and difficult.

Our call, then, is to make sure our own nation reaches out in the right way and on the right side to these troubled spots in the world. And more than this, our call is to start right where we are and rid our thinking of hostility and rancor. That's where it really starts. The Christmas hymn says, "Let every heart prepare him room," and that's our assignment, personally. Not just to be peaceful: Jesus did not say, "Blessed are the peaceful." He said, "Blessed are the *peacemakers*" (Matthew 5:9).

So beginning right at home and extending out through our broader life, each one of us is a piece of the puzzle—and with the right attitude, peace breaks out. It may deal with the way we drive down the freeway at rush hour, or how we deal with a quarrelsome neighbor, or how we respond when someone offends us, but that's where we start being peacemakers. It's often easier to be peacemakers half a world away than it is in our own home or our own community. But still, that's where we start, right here, right now, in attitude and action—peace breaking out right where we live.

We return to my son Steve, and his description of his visit to the Berlin Wall. Friendly Germans pointed the way for him and his friend. They drew nearer, and there it loomed at last. Sure enough, there were jagged gaps in that once impregnable barrier. Strangest of all, pick axes lay here and there on the ground near the Wall. No one seemed to know where they came from but there they were. And every visitor to the Wall was drawn to respond to the unspoken invitation to hoist one of the pick axes and have a go at the Wall himself or herself.

So Steve grabbed a pick and found himself a spot, as others were doing. He joined the tens of thousands who dismantled that symbol of fear and enmity one chunk at a time. Down came one more piece of the Wall, which he is bringing to us next week. Great pieces of the Wall are still standing, but there are picks everywhere. Bit by bit, it's coming down.

Perhaps that describes our assignment: just to find a place at some wall of our own choosing, and do whatever we can to bring a piece of it down. Not so long ago a Jewish soldier named Zev Traum was on patrol in the Gaza Strip in Israel. He was thirty-four. Born in New York City, he had moved to Israel fifteen years ago, gotten married, had children. There in the horrors of Gaza a shot rang out from the shadows, and Zev Traum fell to the ground with a terrible head wound. He was taken to the hospital in Jerusalem, but within a few hours was declared brain dead.

After very hard thought, Zev's wife Brenda found a pick ax. She lifted it, stepped to the wall....

Goodbyes were said to Zev Traum by his wife and three small children in one final moment of tenderness. Then the respirators were turned off. Moments later, Zev Traum's strongly beating, healthy heart was removed and transplanted into the chest of a fifty-four-year-old man—a Palestinian Arab who would die without a transplanted heart. Yet today, that Jewish heart goes on beating and beating and beating in a Palestinian's body. In one more tiny little moment, a piece of the wall comes down, and peace breaks out.

It may be just a matter of attitude for us, or perhaps a small peacemaking act. But this week, see if you can find a pick, and a place at the wall. And if you start chipping away, don't be surprised if you start to hear angels sing:

> Glory to God in the highest heaven,
> and on earth peace among those whom he favors!

13 | *Advent*

Moses: A Child Adrift

Exodus 2:1-10

The moment we get our children, we must start turning loose of them. Physically, a mother first turns loose of her baby when she delivers, and that only begins the process. That first time we leave the baby with a sitter, we turn loose. The first time we leave her in the church nursery, we turn loose. When he gets out of the car to walk uncertainly up to his first day at kindergarten, we sit there and wonder and fret—and turn loose. Inevitably, and so quickly, the time comes when the simple question, "How was school today?" has to be delivered long distance—and we are still turning loose.

So quickly we have to put our children into some poorly woven little basket of experience and set them adrift in a risky world. How is it, then, that we can keep doing this? Knowing how dangerous this world is, how can we keep bringing newborn infants into it?

During this Advent season, leading up to the best known of all birth stories, we will be looking at some biblical stories of parents and their newborn, at mistakes made and achievements accomplished. We will look at the birth of Moses and Samuel and Isaac and Jesus, and hold these stories up to the light to see what God has to say to us—not just as parents but as individuals who have, ourselves, survived being turned loose to make our own way in this turbulent world.

Today's story is set thirty-five hundred years ago in the shadow of the Pyramids, and what child is this that we hear crying among the reeds of the river Nile? It is Moses, born at a time when the Pharaoh was trying to control the Hebrew slaves by having their boy babies killed. A son had been born to a Levite couple, and the mother had hidden her baby for three months. Knowing that she could safely hide him no longer, she made a little basket of bull rushes, daubed it with pitch, set the baby in it, and turned him loose. She set the basket in the reeds along the Nile where Pharaoh's daughter came to bathe. Sure enough, she found the baby, and raised him up to adulthood—and with the rest of Moses' story we are familiar.

As we start the journey toward Christmas, then, what do we see in this story of a child set adrift in an uncertain time?

If you are now or have ever been a parent, surely you sense how Moses' mother must have felt when she set her baby adrift on the waters of the Nile. Oh, the anxiety of parenthood, the fear, the precariousness of every moment of turning loose! Parents do it over and again, a step at a time, setting those little ones adrift out in an unfriendly, often hostile, world. And young parents, especially, are so new at it. God puts the hard job of raising a baby in the hands of two kids who have never done it before, and it all moves so quickly.

Here this little one is, and in so many ways she starts leaving us long before we have woven the basket tightly enough. There is always a little more pitch to be daubed on to make the basket safe. But while we are weaving baskets and mixing pitch they are already leaving, drifting right out through the reeds into a dangerous world. And we know too well what's out there.

The ancient Egyptians had a way of dealing with this, and Egyptian villagers today follow the same strategy. If you were traveling in Egypt today and saw a mother with a brand-new baby, what would be the proper thing to say? If you should say, "What a beautiful baby," the mother most likely would gasp and turn pale—for to compliment a baby calls it to the attention of the spirit of envy, and the baby may be taken away by illness or accident. The proper thing to say on seeing that little one is, "What a horrible little creature! Isn't that the ugliest child you've ever seen?" The mother's face will brighten and she will thank you, and the spirit of envy will leave the child and depart.

We today do not fear the spirit of envy, but we know that there are enemies out there all the same. The ancient mapmakers used to decorate the edges of their maps, out beyond the explored areas of continent and ocean, with fearful pictures and with the words, "Here be dragons!" Out in the unknown of time, out in our children's tomorrows, "here be dragons!"—and their names are Nuclear War and AIDS and Violence and Economic Uncertainty.

Just think of it! We launch our little ones right out into the midst of all of this, and we pay the price. Most of us with teenagers have lain awake at night and heard the midnight sirens wail and we have wondered about the dragons. When our children leave home, we do not pay quite that much attention to the sirens anymore, but we know there are sirens in other towns, and sometimes it causes us to tremble.

From Moses' time to our own, it has been the duty of parents to overcome their anxieties and trust God and God's world enough to start turning loose and see what comes among the reeds of the future to claim them.

Now, is all this bad? Does it mean the pain isn't worth it? Don't risk having children? Not at all! If you wonder whether it is wise to bring a child into the world, ask the same question in regard to your parents. Should they have brought *you* into the world? Was life easy then, back in the turbulent 1920s, the depressed 1930s, the violent 1940s, or the fifties or the sixties? Should they have decided the risks were too great? After all, someone set *you* adrift, someone turned *you* loose, and you have survived quite well!

Or ask the joyous Hebrew slaves a few years later as Moses is leading them out of captivity: "Was it worth it, all the anxiety of Moses' mother?" How foolish of her, to risk having a baby in a slave's world. But there is never a perfect time, a safe time, to risk the future, is there? Halford Luccock once told of the cartoon which pictured

the end of a bridge hand. A bystander is solemnly reprov-
ing the winning couple and saying, "You wouldn't have
won if you'd played it right."

> You can almost elevate that remark to the
> rank of an axiom that those who have made
> the greatest achievements of history would
> not have won if they had "played it
> right"....This is true not only of history but of
> your own life. Your marriage, for instance.
> The chances are that if you had played it
> right, you could not have married when you
> did...the same is true of babies. If a couple
> waits until the absolutely right time to have
> a baby, they find there *is* no convenient time.
> There never was. The greatest baby of all
> was born at a very inconvenient time: The
> parents were on a journey, there was no
> room for them at the Inn. If the parents
> played it absolutely right, with 100 percent
> caution, they never win.[1]

Risk produces life, doesn't it? Most of us see that
whatever muscles we've grown, whatever strength we've
developed, whatever character we've gained, has come
because of struggle—because someone trusted us and God
enough to turn loose, and send us on our way through the
reeds of life.

Suddenly, then, we're not just talking about parents
and their newborn. We are talking about all of us "once and
former infants" who are dealing now with the challenge of
life. For us, right now, the certainties and the uncertainties pull at one another. Back in the past is the security of
mother and father and home, and out there off the edge of
the future are the dragons. The known and the unknown
dance constantly together in our lives, one leading at one
moment, the other at the next.

But that is the wonder of life for us, the meaning that
comes in the struggle. We are God's children, held up by
the twin gifts God gives us: freedom and love. On the one
hand, freedom is there to do as we will with this life—to
take risks, to stumble and fall, to march out into an

uncertain future and take it as an adventure. That kind of freedom God gives us. But on the other hand, God gives also a love that supports us every step of the way. A life that has this faith can move out through the reeds, knowing that the journey ends always with God. Yes, there are many uncertainties. No, we do not know exactly how the journey will run. But faith keeps us risking and trying.

It has often been observed that we go to doctors we don't know, accept prescriptions we cannot read, and take medicines we don't understand. And why? In the midst of ignorance and uncertainty, it is faith that impels and guides us.

And that describes Moses' parents as they set him adrift among the reeds. It describes Moses as he struggled to free his people. It describes David as he fought and Amos as he preached and Jesus as he died. Someone has said that big shots are just little shots who keep on shooting. Keeping on in the midst of uncertainty—that's what it's about. Is this what God is saying to you and me through this story of Moses? Is that what I need most to hear this day? *Keeping on.* Working, risking, loving—but keeping on!

It is never all ease and success for God's children. Life isn't like that. It is a mixture of joy and sorrow, achievement and failure, all surrounded by the love of Christ. How does the Christmas hymn put it? "The hopes and fears of all the years are born in thee tonight!" Fears, yes—but hopes, too. And in the blend of the two, we find life taking on joy and meaning for us.

Not just for our little ones, then, but for ourselves as well: Off beyond the edge of the known, "here be dragons"! Yes. But "here be love" too! So send those little ones out with your love. Cast them adrift, for here among the dragons is thanksgiving and generosity, courage and loyalty, a family and friends, jobs worth doing, grandchildren and retirement—and always even among the dragons the sure faith that God

> will deliver you from the snare of the fowler
> and from the deadly pestilence;
> he will cover you with his pinions,
> and under his wings you will find refuge.
> Psalm 91:3-4

[1]Halford Luccock, *Living Without Gloves.* Oxford University Press, 1957, p. 12.

Samuel: A Burdened Child

1 Samuel 1:1-8, 19-20

The most frequent question parents ask is, "Am I doing a good job?" The question is asked out loud, and it is asked silently, but it keeps being asked. "With these children of mine, what kind of a job am I doing?" And the strange thing is that it is often hard to tell. Even when we know a good bit about the parents' story, we are still not absolutely sure. "Good job?" Or bad?

Here is a biblical story about a mother and her child. You can decide whether it is a good story or a bad one. The mother's name was Hannah; she lived some 1200 years before Christ. Her husband had two wives, and the other wife had borne a number of children. Not Hannah. She was childless, and this devastated her. She felt guilty for her childless state, inadequate, despairing. For years she had wanted a child, had prayed for a child—and then, at last, the child came. She called him Samuel, and her gratitude to God overflowed.

So far, so good—right? But now comes the tricky part. So grateful was Hannah for the birth of her child that she gave him away! When Samuel was three years old, she took him to the shrine where the priest Eli held forth. She deposited little Samuel at Eli's feet and explained. "What I asked, I received," Hannah told him, "and now I lend him

79

to the Lord. For his whole life, he is lent to the Lord" (1 Samuel 1:27-28, NEB). Hannah then returned home, "but the boy remained behind in the service of the Lord under Eli, the priest" (2:11, NEB).

So, how do you feel about this story? Is it a good one or a bad one? To be fair, we must remember that it happened in a very different culture and setting from our own. And we also are aware that in the way that it worked out, the story of Samuel became a vital link in the chain of God's reach for God's people. Yet, we still wonder. Even with all of Hannah's piety and faith, something rings discordantly here.

What is it? Why is it that I breathe a sigh of relief that Hannah wasn't my mother? I think it is because Hannah sent little Samuel out into a big world burdened down with her own issues. According to her own needs, she wrote a script for Samuel and delivered it with him to Eli. What child is this, then, that we hear crying in the temple at Shiloh? It is Samuel, a child burdened down with some parental luggage he was given to cart around for the rest of his life.

Okay, you say, get specific. Exactly what burdens had Hannah put on Samuel?

Her gratitude, first of all. She had wanted a child, wept for a child, prayed for a child—and now she had one. Hannah's gratitude is expressed in the psalm of thanksgiving she offered, in 1 Samuel 2. "My heart exults in the Lord," she said (2:1). And now, curiously, having received this great gift, she hands the bill to Samuel and asks him to pay it. "Samuel," she seemed to say, "I am so grateful to God that I want you to serve God for the rest of your life."

Hannah was not the last one to find someone else to pay for her gratitude. Almost every time our nation is threatened there will always be some who express gratitude by letting someone else go fight for it. Some of us are grateful for our church, but expect someone else to pay for its preservation and its programs. Hannah was grateful and asked Samuel to say "Thank you" for her, with his whole life.

But Samuel also carried much of his mother's feeling of inadequacy. Justly or not, Hannah had felt personally responsible for her childless state. It was the wife's duty and honor in that day to produce as many children as possible, not just for her husband but for her nation. Hannah did not measure up here. She was inadequate, and she was determined that whatever her own weaknesses were, Samuel would be perfect.

So Hannah didn't just take him to Sunday school. She left him there! There is no description of what Eli, the priest, thought when he was suddenly given a three-year-old child to raise up in the service of God. Childcare facilities in Shiloh were bound to be limited, but because Hannah was determined that little Samuel grow up more able than she was, she left him there in Shiloh as a gift to God.

Do children often bear the burden of their parents' feelings of guilt? It is inevitable, isn't it? I like the story about the college freshman who opens up a "care package" from home and finds a note from his mom: "Dear son, I hope you enjoy and appreciate the fruit and cookies I'm sending you. Are you having a good semester? Did you volunteer in class as I suggested? Teachers are always impressed by students who volunteer. It's a sure way to better grades. Remember, better grades now will mean a better graduate school later on. Are you eating well? Proper nutrition is essential to good study. Are you getting enough sleep? Are you making lots of nice new friends?" His roommate walks in, and asks, "What did you get from home?" The frosh answers, "cookies, fruit, and guilt."

If Samuel carried around his mother's gratitude, he also carried her guilt—and that's a big burden for anyone to tote.

But add to this Hannah's ambition for Samuel. Maybe her husband's other wife did have a whole flock of sons and daughters while Hannah had just one son. No matter! Samuel would rise high, and when he did, what would the other says *then* about Hannah? It was a high price to pay, but Hannah packed little Samuel's bags and deposited him at Eli's place in Shiloh nonetheless. They would see what her son would make of himself—to her reflected glory. Ambition for our children is almost always ambition for ourselves, once removed.

How hard it is for any parent to let children live out their own lives. In a poem called "The Generous Heart,"

Jane Merchant describes a woman who did.

> She had a warm and generous heart
> And she had mastered as her own
> The delicate, essential art
> Of letting those she loves alone.

Many of us make the mistake of feeling that the more we love them, the less we can leave them alone. So we burden them down with all sorts of second-hand dreams and inherited ambition, and never do learn the art of "letting those we love alone."

Charlie Shedd puts it this way: "Blessed is the family where children are allowed to become what they can as fast as they can. Blessed also are the parents who, as fast as they can, will get out of the way."[1]

The story of Hannah and Samuel gives us a faint feeling of uneasiness because when Hannah packed Samuel's bags, she loaded it down with much of her own gratitude, her own guilt, and her own ambition. And that's a pretty big burden for anyone to carry.

And how did it all turn out? That's one of the redeeming and relieving graces of parenthood. It turned out pretty well, as it often does, despite Hannah's mistakes. Samuel grew up to be a great prophet, playing an essential role in the selection of Saul as Israel's first king, and then of David, the unifier of the nation. Samuel bore his burdens well. He was gruff but good, cantankerous but conscientious, self-righteous but decent. Samuel was one of those who would never have been missed at the office party; in fact, people would have a better time if he were not there. Yet, despite his mother's burdens, he did his own part in helping to fulfill God's reach for God's people.

To parents, it may simply mean that we ought to relax with our frantic, worried parenting. Even if with all good intentions we make mistakes, probably some good will come of it.

On a trip to Chicago recently, I sat next to a woman who tried to keep her unruly two-year-old ruly, without much success. The child was impossible. Finally, the mother swatted the girl on the bottom, pointed to the emergency door and the flight attendant, and said, "See that door? That's where they throw people out of the airplane if they don't behave themselves." The little girl continued unruly, but I behaved myself the rest of the flight, I assure you. When parents try to do a good job, the fallout is usually good, even when mistakes are made.

And to all of us grown-up infants, busily trying to arrange our own lives and at the same time keep on carrying some of our parents' burdens: What does it say to us? It says *we can't keep blaming the Hannahs all our lives for our own predicaments.* Our mothers and our fathers did burden us down with all sorts of things. But that's just the way parenting works. They had no other option. They had nothing else to give us but themselves, frail and flawed. But that doesn't mean we have to carry their luggage the rest of our lives, does it? At any moment, Samuel could have laid down Hannah's burdens and gone his own way. And so can any of us.

Some of us ease so gently through adolescence into adulthood that we never realize that the chains are not put there by our parents but by ourselves—that we are free human beings, free to keep carrying those burdens or free to lay them down. Enough, then, of this modern tendency to blame what we are on someone else. It is a part of the freedom we receive in Christ Jesus, to take on responsibility for the person that we become.

I read somewhere about the woman who realized at the last moment that she had not sent out her Christmas cards. She had forty-nine names on her list. So she ran to the card shop, saw a package of fifty cards with a nice Christmas picture on the front, bought them, rushed back home, addressed and stamped the envelopes, quickly signed the cards, and ran to the post office and mailed them. Returning home relaxed after getting this last-minute job speedily done, she saw the one remaining card lying on the table. She idly picked it up to read finally the verse on the inside. It said, "This simple card is just to say a little gift is on its way"!

Parenting is a matter of promising a lot of little gifts. Some are appropriate and some are burdensome, and some are never sent. Hannah had some gifts that fit all three categories, and with all her mistakes her burdened child turned out well. For all of us parents of children, and all us children of parents, that's splendid good news!

[1]Charles Shedd, *Promises to Peter.* Word Books, 1970, p. 20.

15 | *Advent*

Isaac: A Child Called Laughter

Genesis 21:1-6

"What shall we name the new baby?" It's a frequent question. In a way, it's easier for us than it was for ancient people. In much earlier days, names were given that had a specific meaning—which was especially unfortunate for children of the ancient prophets. Their dads were always making preaching points with the names bestowed.

Hosea, who had good reason to doubt the faithfulness of his wife Gomer, called his daughter Lo-ruhamah, which means "not loved." He named his son Lo-ammi, which means "not my people." Isaiah named one of his sons Maher-shalal-hash-baz, which means "the spoil speeds, the prey hastens."

"What shall we name the baby?" Sarah and Abraham did not have to debate the question long. "Let's call him Laughter," they said, and that's exactly what they did. The word in Hebrew is "Isaac," and Isaac became the patriarch who stood between his father, Abraham, and his son, Jacob.

Why Laughter? Because Sarah and Abraham had been without children, and long after the natural childbearing age had passed, Sarah became pregnant and Isaac was born. "God has brought laughter for me," Sarah said; "everyone who hears will laugh with me" (Genesis 21:6).

86

What was more natural, then, than to express the incredible joy she felt by naming the child Laughter.

Sometimes in the midst of our often grim and unsmiling search for absolute obedience and strict righteousness and correct belief, Sarah's strategy comes as a needed corrective. What some homes need even more than more righteousness is more joy! Of course, joy and laughter are often like lost dogs that only come home when we quit looking for them. Nonetheless, we chase happiness much like a little kid chasing a ball: The instant we catch up to it, we kick it away. Sarah devised a strategy for keeping around at least a reminder of what God wills for God's people. She named her baby Isaac. He was a child called Laughter.

On the wall of my study is an Egyptian papyrus that pictures the last judgment. According to their idea, at the moment of judgment, the god Osiris would ask each person two questions to determine whether or not the individual could continue on the journey to the afterlife. The questions were, "Did you bring joy?" and "Did you find joy?"

In the Advent season, it is particularly appropriate for us to do a little searching here, and see how much joy and laughter we've managed to accumulate. And why so?

It is thoroughly biblical. The Egyptian Osiris was not the only voice calling for joy as an essential of life. Such claims exist over and again in our Bible. Consider the recurring rhythm in the Psalms, for example.

Make a joyful noise to the Lord, all the earth.
Worship the Lord with gladness (100:1-2a).

Break forth into joyous song and sing praises....
Let the floods clap their hands;
let the hills sing together for joy (98:4b, 8).

Then our mouth was filled with laughter,
and our tongue with shouts of joy (126:2a).

That same spirit is echoed by Jesus: "You will have pain [now], but your pain will turn into joy" (John 16:20b). "Ask and you will receive, so that your joy may be complete" (John 16:24). And when he described the entering of the faithful into heaven, he put it like this: "Well done, good and trustworthy [servant]...enter into the joy of your master" (Matthew 25:21).

No one who takes the Bible seriously should apologize for making life joyful and laughter filled, because the Bible continually describes this as one of the characteristics of God's people. Whether it is a child or a father or a mother, someone needs to be named Laughter at your house and mine, because it is thoroughly biblical.

A second reason is that laughter and joy bring us strength. Exactly how this works may be uncertain, but the saying is indeed true: They who laugh, last! Gloom uses up strength. Joy produces it. It is no accident, no coincidence, that one of the first and strongest symptoms of depression is utter fatigue. The clinically depressed person hardly has the strength to begin each day. As depression is lessened, strength begins to return.

Several years ago, Norman Cousins survived a severe heart attack. In his book, *Anatomy of an Illness*, he described how important laughter and joy were in his move back toward renewed health. Indeed, following his observations, some hospitals for chronically ill patients have now set up "laugh rooms" where humorous periodicals and books and movies can be used by worn-out patients, with remarkable results. How striking it is to observe this modern development in medicine and then read a three-thousand-year-old verse from Proverbs that proclaims,

A cheerful heart is a good medicine,
     but a downcast spirit dries up the bones (17:22).

It is surely true at your house and at mine that when things go badly and no one is very happy with anyone else and all is tension and despair, what we need then is not more dogged righteousness or more strict obedience or more disciplined Bible study. What we need is a healthy dose of what God offers us in abundance: more joy, more laughter.

I knew an older woman in a church I served down in Texas, a woman with a remarkable gift for cheering up whoever came to visit her. One day we talked about how we endure and overcome our times of ill health and loneliness, and she wrote out for me a little poem she had found somewhere, one which she said had become her road map for her later years. She did not know who its author was, but here are the words she wrote, the words of a poem-prayer:

> God, keep my heart attuned to laughter
>   when youth is done,
> When all the days are gray days,
>   coming after the warmth, the sun.
> God, keep me then from bitterness,
>   from grieving, when life seems cold.
> God, keep me always joyful, and believing,
>   as I grow old.

We should not imply that it is easy. It wasn't for her, and it isn't for others either. But it's a prayer that can be answered. And life, even in the later days, can have that trademark of joy about it.

An old, retired professor of church history at Yale is best remembered for the last words he uttered. He was on his deathbed, his anxious relatives gathered round, waiting for the certain inevitability. After a time of silence, one of the relatives quietly said, "I think he's gone." Another relative, standing at the end of the bed, felt the old man's feet and said, "No, his feet are still warm. No one ever dies with warm feet." Whereupon the old church history professor raised his head up from the bed and said, "Joan of Arc did," gave a little chuckle, and died.

Laughter and joy give us strength for the journey, and enable us to run the race to its end.

But even more, laughter and joy give a spirit to life that makes *it worth living*. This Advent season, how much we need that, yet how persistently it eludes us. I suppose that one of the most frequently violated verses in the entire Bible is Psalm 118:24:

> This is the day that the Lord has made;
>   let us rejoice and be glad in it.

And strangely, the more earnestly some folk take religion, the more they violate this verse. Many a person who first begins to think seriously about Jesus Christ and his claim on life turns into a sour-faced searcher for evil in this world. After suffering one of her abusive harangues, Charlie Brown asked Lucy—the haranguer—what on earth he could do about it. Lucy replied, "I don't give advice. I merely point out the trouble."

Lucy's cousins in this world are legion. Some of the most dedicated Christians believe earnestly that God has appointed them special agents in charge of pointing out the trouble! Their friends' faith isn't quite good enough, the church isn't quite good enough, the music isn't quite good enough. Like those immense black holes out in space that absorb even the nearby light, these earnest folk capture and absorb any stray joy that happens near.

In New York City I saw many magnificent sights, but the one that sticks out in my mind was the panel truck whizzing down Fifth Avenue with the company name on the side: The J and E Pigeon Eliminating Company. Imagine that—an entire company designed for the exclusive purpose of eliminating pigeons. I could imagine as that truck sped so fast down Fifth Avenue that somewhere a crisis existed, and a pigeon was about to be eliminated.

In Jesus' day, the Pharisees had informally organized themselves into the Joy Eliminating Company. Imagine how they felt when here came Jesus saying, "I have said these things to you so that my joy may be in you, and that your joy may be complete" (John 15:11). It begins to be more understandable that the Pharisees soon reorganized themselves into the Jesus Eliminating Company, and Calvary came near.

The Christian today needs to work in the other direction, and become the Joy Producing Company—at home, at church, at work, wherever. One of my favorite writers is Erma Bombeck, and I have always enjoyed the way she describes her strategy late in the afternoon when she knows her husband will soon be home from the office. She knows that the first thing he will do when he comes in the front door will be to take a deep sniff to see what's cooking in the kitchen. So, she says, when he's due home in twenty minutes and she hasn't the faintest notion of what's for dinner, she goes to the cupboard and pulls out a lone onion, turns the oven on, and plops the onion inside. You know what happens. In about fifteen minutes, the house is filled with the wonderful aroma of that onion in the oven. When her husband comes in the front door, he takes a deep breath, smiles in satisfaction, and heads for the evening news, giving Erma time to figure out what on earth she's going to fix for dinner that evening.

In a roundabout sort of way, there ought to be an onion in the oven at home or at church all the time, so that when people first come in the door, they can sense it immediately—a warmth, a fragrance. This is a joyful place. This is a place where people love one another. This is a family here. There is a faith here that has produced joy and laughter, and Jesus' prayer is being fulfilled: "I have said these things to you so that...your joy may be complete" (John 15:11). How, again, did Osiris put it? Did you find joy? Did you give joy? Then enter into the Kingdom.

Sarah and Abraham named their child Laughter, and though there is no other reference to it in Isaac's story, it must have flavored that family's life together from then on. As we continue our approach toward Christmas and the celebration of the birth of Jesus—whose name means "God brings salvation"!—may there be someone in your home and in your family of faith whose name, whose life, means laughter and joy.

16 | *Advent*

Jesus: Child of Mystery

Luke 2:15-20

It's a different birth story—that of Jesus—than those of Samuel or Isaac. Their parents had yearned for a child, prayed for a child. Long years had passed before a child was born, to their great delight. Not so with Mary and Joseph. They obviously didn't really want a child, didn't plan on a child, and yet, embarrassingly early, a child was on the way.

Jesus came surrounded by mystery, and mystery hovered around him throughout his extraordinary life and unusual death. Always, from the beginning, there was the hint that more was there than met the eye. Hidden away were meaning and truth that stayed just off stage.

Why a baby, to begin with? From the outset, the proposition was that this child was God's son, the long-awaited Messiah. But when the ancient ones talked of a coming Messiah, a baby in a crib was most definitely not what they expected. As the poet describes it,

> They were all looking for a king
>   To slay their foes and lift them high;
> Thou cam'st, a little baby thing
>   That made a woman cry.[1]

The mystery is enlarged by the ancient claim that Jesus' birth was unusual in that it was no human union that conceived the child. Two of the four gospels make the claim (Matthew 1:22-23; Luke 1:27). Mary was a virgin, and Jesus was, quite literally, God's son. Although the doctrine of the virgin birth was not ever referred to by Jesus himself, nor by the gospels of Mark or John, and is not mentioned anywhere else in all the New Testament, still it came to be, from early on, a central article of Christian faith.

For some, it is a mandatory belief, one without which a person cannot really be a Christian. For others, of equally sincere faith, it is one of the many details of Jesus' life that enhance, but do not authenticate, Jesus' identity as God's son. There are people of good faith who look at this particular mystery from a number of different vantage points.

Some of us accept it without blinking. Others of us, children of a scientific, rational age, almost automatically reject any idea which has an element of miracle about it. The tendency to be skeptical and disbelieve anything that has the nature of miracle about it is basically a product of human pride. We don't want God doing anything that we cannot do!

A number of years ago, there was an old professor at Harvard Divinity School who was being subjected to considerable ridicule because of his belief in the virgin birth of Jesus. This teaching was regarded as a naive myth by many of his younger colleagues. One day one of them challenged the old man for holding what was regarded as an intellectually irresponsible position. The younger man said, "Do you mean to tell me that if some young woman from Boston came into the hospital and said that she was going to have a baby, that she was a virgin, and that an angel had appeared to her, you would believe her?"

The old man hesitated, thought for a long while, and then answered, slowly: "No, I probably wouldn't believe her story. I would probably dismiss her words. But I'll tell you one thing for sure. If that baby grew up to manhood and his teachings changed the course of history, if he grew up and eventually died on a cross and rose from the dead, if two thousand years later fully one-third of the world's

population called him Savior and Lord—if that happened,
I think I would give that girl's story a second hearing!"

It's a mystery worth thinking about, isn't it? The old
philosopher once said that stars were made to twinkle, not
to study. So with some ideas like the virgin birth: Analyze
it endlessly, study it earnestly, dissect it completely, and
its truth utterly dies away. But through its mystery, it
twinkles with truth.

But as Jesus grew up, there is an added mystery. Think
of it! Every person saw in him just what they needed to
make their life meaningful and complete. The ancient
explorer, Marco Polo, tells of a Persian village from which,
so the villagers claimed, the three kings had started on
their journey to Bethlehem. Strangely, they said, when the
three arrived at the manger, the young king found a young
Christ. The middle-aged king found a Savior of his own
age. And the old king found an old companion.

It's a strange story that Marco Polo brought back, and
yet this is what we see when we look at Jesus' life. What a
wide variety of people came to him, and whatever their
need they found the blank spots of their lives being filled
by Jesus. There was Simon Peter, unpredictable and
impetuous, becoming the rock on which Jesus built his
church. There was the woman caught in adultery, finding
in Jesus forgiveness and a way to start over.

And indeed, isn't this what happens every Sunday
morning when we come to worship? Just look at us! What
an incredible variety of people and conditions and needs
we represent! Some of us are smart as a whip, and some of
us are slow to understand. Some of us have graduate
degrees in Bible knowledge and others of us are kinder-
gartners. Some of us are so adept at prayer that the words
slip out like boiled okra and others of us can't get the first
croaking words out. Some of us are young and just beginning
and others of us are nearing the end of our exciting journey.
Some of us are good and others of us feel in all honesty that
we are just plain bad!

But here we are, and Jesus sits right beside each one of
us at this moment, doling out forgiveness to some of us,
encouragement to others. For some of us he hands out self-
esteem and affirmation, and to others of us he fills the

spoon with a dollop of humility and urges us to swallow it. But whatever our need is today, we find the answer in the remarkable gospel that he brings to us, if we can just see it.

How does this work? That's a part of the mystery too, the indirection of God. How indirectly God does fill in the blanks of our lives, if we will just set ourselves to the task of following Jesus and living the best we can. In the quest of following Jesus, these needs are met.

Kansans are justly proud of the story of the Wizard of Oz, but it may well have dimensions many of us have never recognized. Frederick Buechner has pointed out that the story is a remarkable parable telling how God works through Christ.

Remember the outline of the story? Blown away by a tornado, Dorothy sets out to find the Wizard who, she believes, can help her get home again. She is joined on the way by a Cowardly Lion, who wants courage; a Tin Woodsman, who wants a heart; and a Scarecrow, who wants a brain.

But remarkably, in the course of their journey, each begins to find what he is seeking. Every time danger arises, the Cowardly Lion stumbles ahead with his growing courage. Every time a problem arises, the Scarecrow manages to figure a way out of it. And of all this interesting quartet, it is the apparently "heartless" Tin Woodsman who weeps so profusely at the misfortune of others that an oilcan must be used to keep his tears from rusting him into immobility. At the journey's end, they discover that they have found what they were looking for. Remember Robert Louis Stevenson's words? "To travel hopefully is better than to arrive."

Enough, then, of this constant human tendency to see the fulfillment of all our dreams in some far-away destination, some moment of arrival somewhere at which point I will only *then* be the person I want to be and intend to be. Buechner warns us clearly that this day just does not come this way for most of us.

It has never come, simply because they did not understand that courage is his who with

his scalp cold with fear, yet acts coura-
geously. A brain, a real brain, is his who
knows that he is as much a fool as a Scarecrow, yet manages somehow to do all a
Scarecrow can. A heart is his who is willing
to let it be broken. For us, the one who
confronts us with ourselves and with this
truth is not a wizard at all, but God who
addresses us through his son, Jesus.[2]

It will never leave us, this aspect of mystery. It is this
indirection of God's strategy that continues to amaze us,
the incongruity of it all. How can a crib bring salvation?
How can a cross bring eternal life? The dimension, the
impact of Christmas for us will always depend on our
ability to see God's gifts coming through the side doors of
our lives, while we are not looking.

I remember a Christmas time many years ago when
one of my sons was a fourth grader. He came into my office
at the church one afternoon shortly before Christmas and
asked if there was any job he could do for me. Two hours,
maybe. His Sunday school teacher had suggested that this
was a gift each of the children could give their parents, and
these two hours of work would be his gift to me. His eyes
glowed with excitement. It would be something he could do
for me!

I tried to think of what it might be. I remembered that
someone had just given me a package of 250 beautiful
bookplates with my name embossed, all gummed on the
back for sticking inside my books. Would he be interested
in sticking these bookplates inside the front covers of my
books? Sure he would. When could he start? "What about
right now?" I said. I was about to go hospital visiting for a
couple of hours. Where should he start, top shelf or bottom?
"Start anywhere," I said, "just put one bookplate inside
each front cover." And I was gone.

Two hours later I was back, and he had finished. "There
weren't nearly enough bookplates," he said. He had only
finished two shelves, and the bookplates were gone. What
had gone wrong? "Start anywhere," I had said, and he had
started on the shelf that held only a collection of several
years' subscriptions to half a dozen religious journals.

Methodically, faithfully, neatly, he had stuck inside the
front cover of each of those magazines one of the precious
bookplates, and so had run out of them long before he got
to any books at all!

Isn't it a mystery? If he had done the job the ordinary
way, I would never have remembered it, but whenever I
pick up one of these old journals and find a bookplate
carefully placed inside, I remember the glow in a small
boy's eyes, and the love that put it there.

It's a mystery, yes. On Christmas morn you will no
doubt unwrap some beautiful packages, but if you want to
find the real gift, look inside the front covers of some of the
journals of your life and you will find them. It wasn't in the
palace of Jerusalem that the gift was given but, strangely,
mysteriously, inside the front cover of a manger at
Bethlehem. When we see it every year, we remember the
glow in God's eyes, and the love that put it there.

How did the poet say it, once again?

> They were all looking for a king
> To slay their foes and lift them high;
> Thou cam'st, a little baby thing
> That made a woman cry.

[1]George Macdonald, "That Holy Thing."
[2]Frederick Buechner, *The Magnificent Defeat*. Harper & Row,
1966, p. 34.

17

Christmas Sunday

A Two-King Christmas

Matthew 2:1-12

It was the night of the Christmas pageant, and a quick decision had to be made. The young people were putting on the pageant, and actors for the main parts had long since been selected and rehearsed. There was, of course, a Mary and a Joseph and a Cabbage Patch Jesus. There were some bathrobed shepherds, and a chorus of angels. From the youth choir, the three boys who could carry a tune had been identified and selected for the most important role. They were to be the three kings. As a glorious conclusion to the pageant they would parade down the center aisle, not only carrying gifts to lay at the feet of the holy family, but also they would sing as they walked, "We three kings of Orient are; bearing gifts we traverse afar, field and fountain, moor and mountain, following yonder star." It would be the high point of the Christmas pageant.

Now, shepherds and angels and holy family were all arrived and in place. But disaster struck. One of the three kings, late that afternoon, had been diagnosed as having a case of the mumps. It was too late to find a replacement at all, much less one who could sing. The two remaining kings and their harried director stood frantically discussing what to do. The musical overtures to Christmas were already sounding, the crowds were gathering. The time for

97

Christmas joy had come, and they all realized that it was
not going to go as they had hoped and planned. Despite all
their careful work, their rehearsings and yearning, the
moment had arrived and they were one king short. What
could they do? What would *you* have done?

An appropriate question, because it describes a predicament most of us experience in a symbolic sort of way
when Christmas rolls around. Despite a lot of planning
and some hard work and sheer determination, few of us
come to Christmas with the cast of our lives intact and all
the props in place. Maybe quite literally, someone who has
always played a central role in our lives is now gone, and
while we thought we had come to terms with that, all the
soft sounds open the old wounds, and we feel it over again.
Or maybe it is some other unexpected problem. We know
that Christmas is supposed to be such a happy time. But
in the midst of it, some distant memory stirs itself, and,
quite against our will, we remember battles we lost with
ourselves, hopes that didn't pan out, dreams that disin-
tegrated right before us. There are very few of us who do
not come to Christmas with a king or two missing. We, too,
face the same question:What do we do now?

One option, of course, was to cancel the pageant altogether, or at least the kings. Although the scripture nowhere tells us how many kings, or wise men, there were,
tradition has always said that there were three of them.
They were even given names: Gaspar, Melchoir, and
Balshazar. Three kings, everyone knows that there were
three kings. If we can't have a complete set, the pageant
director may have thought, let us have none. So wipe the
makeup off those two young faces, fold up the striped
bathrobes, put aside Grandpa's cane, and cancel the kings
altogether. If there can't be three, let there be none.

It is certainly a possible response to these "two-king"
Christmases most of us face. Something has gone wrong,
something unexpected has come up, someone is missing, it
didn't work out, the incense has spoiled, the gold is tar-
nished, the report was bad, she wasn't accepted, he didn't
get the job—and with all this disappointing reality,
Christmas comes limping in with too much missing. So the
solution suggests itself: Forget it!

It happens more than we might know, this resigned rejection not just of Christmas but of the myriad good—the fresh, hopeful spirit—that Christmas stands for. Something is missing, someone is singing out of key, so what's the point of my stubborn song? It infects us in so many different levels of life, from the incidental and the trivial to the momentous.

• Why should I straighten up the house, when no one else even hangs their clothes up or picks their towels up off the bathroom floor?

• Is there any reason why I should give to support the church, when so many others don't give anything?

• Why should I be faithful in a world where unfaithfulness is a national pastime?

• What's the point of any effort toward personal purity and decency when filth is well stocked and selling fast?

• Why should I keep talking of peace in a world where the word itself makes people mad, where we bicker over almost everything, where there is so much poorly disguised hatred about?

You see the easy temptation running through it all? If the cast isn't complete and the set perfect, then forget the commitment and cancel the celebration. In a previous life, I used to play bridge with a group of fellows who went at it furiously. One partner in particular kept the game exciting. His theory of bridge was that any hand had at least a fifty-fifty chance of making game, so he never bid part scores. He kept bidding and bidding until a game was reached, and down, down, down we would usually go. He has many cousins among us, persons who do not recognize that real life is made up of a lot of part scores, games not quite made, play-offs missed, shadowed victories, muted songs, family dinners with a chair or two empty.

One option we face, as did the pageant director, was this: If we can't have it all this Christmas, we'll have nothing. So you bring the "bah," and I'll bring the "humbug." Cancel the celebration, de-wing the angels, call off the pageant. For us, it's three kings or none at all!

There was a second option, for the two kings and their director: Why not simply ignore the fact that there wasn't a third king present? Let the two boys march down the aisle stubbornly keeping to the original script. "We three kings of Orient are," the two boys could sing, and hope that there wouldn't be too many undercurrents of laughter from those among the cast who could count to three.

It is a notch above canceling it altogether, to be sure, and it becomes the strategy of some of us who come to Christmas with a king or two missing. It's a "let's pretend" Christmas. For an hour or two, as the candles flicker and the songs are sung, let's pretend that we didn't say that to each other last week. Let's pretend that there are no cold and hungry people not far away in our city. Let's pretend that these empty places within, or beside, ourselves do not exist. Let's pretend that below the concrete domes, the antiseptic missiles do not lie sleeping, ticking, waiting, poised, ready. Let's pretend that nothing's amiss in this aching old world.

And there is something to be said for a bit of Christmas pretending, even though it sometimes carries us a long way from reality. During the years we lived in San Juan, Puerto Rico, Christmas was always a challenge to us. To buoy up our spirits, we always went to the beach on Christmas day, and sent picture postcards back to our stateside friends. How great, we would write, to spend Christmas day on a sunny beach. Lying in the sun, with the Caribbean waters lapping at our feet. How great!

We may have fooled them, but back to our house we would go and turn on the little oscillating fan, and sit there in 85-degree temperatures, listening to the record player sound out, "Sleigh bells ring, are you listening? In the lane, snow is glistening." And we would get out our slides of previous Christmases in Connecticut. We would decorate our poor, wilted Christmas tree that had been cut in Oregon months before and shipped through the Panama Canal for the benefit of us Yankees. And in that tropical, lush setting, we would dream of a white Christmas—and pretend.

"We three kings of Orient are," the two boys might have sung, ignoring the reality of someone missing, something absent. It fits the advice that William James once gave: "If you wish to possess a qualification or an emotion, act 'as if' you already had it." It's good advice for those of us whose habit is to be negative and fault finding and gloomy. For goodness' sake, for the benefit of everyone else, can't you just *pretend* to be happy? Even if the tie is the wrong color, and the dressing too dry, can't you just pretend? It may be the best gift you can give to your family, the one they would appreciate the most, a bit of convincing pretending. And it may even change you. It is a lot easier to act your way into a new way of thinking than to think your way into a new way of acting.

It was an option for the boys at the Christmas pageant, a bit of stubborn pretense, and there is no doubt that is was better than canceling the celebration altogether. But was there for them, and is there for us, a still better way?

There was—and there is.

The last-second decision was made, whispered instructions were hurriedly given. Step by step now, it came into place. Mary and Joseph edged hesitantly into the stable, and the elementary angels circled behind, singing their song, and then the junior-high shepherds knelt by the manger. And so it came to pass that the pair of now-confident wise men, right on their cue, stepped briskly down the center aisle, singing lustily: "We two kings of Orient are; bearing gifts we traverse afar, field and fountain, moor and mountain, following yonder star."

"*We two kings,*" the two of them sang, and the audience of family and friends smiled knowingly. One and all, they accepted and celebrated their two-king Christmas.

And isn't it the best way for us, as well? No need to cancel Christmas. No need, either, to pretend that all is perfect and in place this holy week. If there is a king or two missing for you this Christmas, then say it, and celebrate anyway.

Perhaps I'm talking to myself here. My daughter won't be here for Christmas for the first time in our life this season. She will be in Indianapolis with *his* family. I know that where to spend Christmas is always a hard decision for young families. I know that!

Knowing it, I had made what seemed to me to be a perfectly reasonable suggestion to Deborah and Brad when they were first married. Do it evenly, I proposed. Come to our house for Christmas and Thanksgiving for the first twenty-five years you are married, and then go to theirs for the next twenty-five. Or I was willing to go even further. Consider all the national holidays, I said, and spend Labor Day, Memorial Day, Columbus Day, Martin Luther King's birthday, and Veterans Day with them, and Christmas and Thanksgiving with us! Nothing worked. They are in Indianapolis this Christmas. A king is missing.

For most of us, someone's missing, something is askew and malfunctioning and quite out of order, and those with a bit of spirit simply acknowledge it and accept it. And go on singing: "We two kings of Orient are." So many of us are, and that scaled-down song is being sung far more often than we might imagine. In a small apartment somewhere, someone who couldn't get home for Christmas is singing it. In a hospital waiting room, someone is singing it, and a soldier in the Aleutians is singing it. A coach who didn't make the play-offs is singing it. So is a fellow looking for work, and a sixteen-year-old girl who wishes someone would call her, and a college sophomore dreading the day his parents get his grades in the mail, and a husband and wife who know they are fitting together rather poorly. They are doing it all around us, maybe sitting right next to us, these stubborn singers of songs and seers of joy and hearers of music, all those who take note of the one-winged angels and tattered shepherds and missing kings and still go on with the celebration.

And that is precisely the point of Christmas! If there weren't a lot of kings missing, and love missing, and hope missing in our world, there would be no need for Christ to come at all. He came to an imperfect world where prejudice abounds, where hostages are taken and held, where famine spreads, where diplomats in dark suits make easy decisions that sentence ten thousand young men to instant death. That's the kind of world he came to, and that's precisely why he came, to bring light to that kind of darkness. And that's why he comes today to you and me, because we too have our own private little store of disappointments.

So don't let the simplicity of the solution throw you off. There is time between now and Christmas day to count the kings who *are* present, to recognize how much good is still real in our lives. It will be our turn, then, to stride right down the center aisle in celebration of our own two-king Christmas.